FOR LOSERS
AND COWARDS

BARBARA BROKHOFF

FOR LOSERS AND COWARDS

ISBN 0-89536-272-4

PRINTED IN U.S.A.

TO

    "MY JOHN"
    husband,
      lover,
        teacher,
          preacher,
            friend,
              and the man I just can't beat at tennis!

TABLE OF CONTENTS

A WOMAN PREACH? A BISHOP SPEAKS

It took a heavenly vision to reveal to the Apostle Peter that, truly, God shows no partiality in bestowing the gifts of ministry. When God manifested his presence and power in the home of Cornelius, there was no longer any doubt in the great Apostle's mind that the Holy Spirit blesses persons of any nation and shows no partiality.
— Acts 10:34-35

The history of Christian thought, ministry, and mission clearly points to this total impartiality as God bestows gifts of ministry upon persons of any age, race, or sex. The great spiritual classics would be prime manifestations of the Holy Spirit working in the lives of women.

God in his graces has bestowed special gifts of ministry upon Barbara Brokhoff. Those of us who have shared in her maturity in faith and ministry for a long time recognize these gifts as marvelous manifestations of God's grace and thank God for her faithful and devoted response to an obvious call to preach.

Her first appointment in the United Methodist Church could only be described as a "hard-scrabble", a rural circuit which no one else would consider serving. Her gifts in that place built a strong parish and soon she was called to a new and larger field covering an entire county in north Missouri. Here God blessed her with increasing ministry and soon she was called to serve an even larger town and country parish.

Barbara is the first to give God the glory for any ministry she has ever been given. But, when I consider the gifts of the Spirit which have given power and compassion to her preaching, I have to say that God blessed her with genuine attractiveness in appearance, in personality, in spiritual depth, and in Christian empathy. She has been given a gift of intellect which enables her to preach with total honesty and clarity. She has been blessed with a deep and sincere humility which has never enabled her to seek position or recognition.

Believe me, dear Reader, it is not my purpose to magnify these gifts but only to say with genuine affection and admiration, A WOMAN CAN PREACH!

Bishop Eugene M. Frank,
formerly Bishop of the Missouri Area,
United Methodist Church

Foreword

A WOMAN PREACH?

In a recent revival, where I was the visiting evangelist-preacher, a certain lady was responsible for filling a certain pew each night of the meeting. Her assigned pew was a front row, not the favorite seating place of most people! One man, whom she had conned into attending the service, entered the church, saw his seat for the evening, saw the speaker, and beginning to realize all of the implications said; "You only invited me to come to church — you didn't tell me they would take an offering, that I had to sit in a front row, and that the preacher was a *WOMAN!* Take me away quick!" Such is one of the many and varied responses that I have encountered in my more than twenty years of ministry in the United Methodist Church.

A lot of questions have been asked down through these years, but the most basic, often-asked question is: *"Why did you decide to be a preacher?"* The answer sounds simplistic, even to me, but it is the absolute truth and basis for being what I am: *I AM A PREACHER BECAUSE GOD CALLED ME TO PREACH, AND I ANSWERED HIS CALL.* (I admit that calling ME to preach may well have been the one mistake God ever made. I have absolutely no idea why he called me, only the firm conviction that he did.)

Then there are other (usually) well-meaning, well-intentioned questions like:
What are the disadvantages of being a woman preacher?
How do "men" preachers treat you?
How can you preach when the Bible says for women to "keep silence in the church?"

What about women taking "authority" over men?
Do you think women should preach?

The following answers to these questions are neither scholarly nor profound, but they are my answers — I would not for a moment presume to answer for others who have answered the call to preach, male or female.

What are the disadvantages of being a woman preacher?

I suppose, truthfully, there are some disadvantages (just as there are definite advantages). A male preacher may also work under disadvantages: he is labeled "too young, too old, too conservative, too liberal, too many children, not married, wrong color," etc. But he manages to work with whatever "Disadvantage" is his, and is the man of God, anyway. So, sometimes I am the "wrong sex" but, God arranged to let me be the minister of God anyway.

Most people are happy to be served, by either sex, so long as they are truly *served*. When the needs of people are met, they usually are not overly-critical of the hand that helps them. Service and performance speak pretty clearly to everybody.

Opportunities for service have come to me far more often than I have deserved. I have probably not always been given equal consideration with men in positions of appointment, but I have always been given more to do than one human (male or female) could get done.

Inequity in monetary payment for my services has been obvious. I could cite many instances, but to illustrate: one church which was using the services of my preacher-husband and me as interim pastors for a month, until their new pastor arrived, paid my husband on his preaching Sundays exactly twice as much as they paid me. If I put a price on the Gospel, and "charged" for my services in the ministry, I'd have to howl loudly at this piece of injustice!

How do "men" preachers treat you?

Great! Other pastors treated me as co-equal when I served the church as a pastor. Now that I serve it as a preaching evangelist, they treat me equally well. They have not been critical or condescending. They have not isolated me, nor ever given the appearance of only "tolerating" me. My brethren in the ministry are my loyal supporters, staunch allies, and my dear friends.

How can you preach when the Bible says for women to "keep silence in the church?"

My literalist friends are deeply troubled by this passage, but totally inconsistent in their practice of keeping the letter of the law. If "silence" means silence — then it obviously means no speaking for any reason — which prohibits prayer, teaching, singing, even a warm "Good Morning," — and who do you know who carries that out?

To better understand what Paul had in mind needs an awareness of the culture and situation of his day. Women of that time were held in pretty low esteem. Few of them had knowledge of social graces, they did not know how to conduct themselves in public, most of them could neither read nor write (many men could not, for that matter), so when the early Christians gathered to hear the teaching/preaching of Paul they sat (usually) men apart from the women, separated often by a wall, curtain, or partition. Thus, when Paul said something a woman did not understand she'd call across to her husband for clarification, then another would address her husband, then another would get into the act, the husbands would try to reply and chaos and confusion was the natural result. So, simply for expediency, to keep order, Paul said: "Women, keep quiet in church — so that this exhortation may continue, you save your questions and ask your husbands when you get home." (Simple, isn't it? Makes sense, doesn't it?)

But — in answering the above question, the immediate response is usually:

What about women taking authority over men?

I really do have some definite convictions about this one. My understanding of the Word is that men are given a role of authority (providing they meet the proper conditions) as well as the women. This does not mean that women are not equals with men, nor does it mean they are in any way inferior to men, but there is a place of submission for women that runs all through the Word of God that is pretty hard for me to deny.

God, however, has called women to roles of leadership both in the Old and New Testaments. Note, for instance, that Hulda was a prophetess and Deborah was one of the judges in Israel.

I love to remember that Philip had five daughters who prophesied (to prophesy means to "tell forth" or to preach).

Remember also that in Acts it says that "in the last days I will pour out my Spirit upon all flesh and your sons and your *daughters* shall prophesy. (Women preachers again.)

And one of the nicest things Jesus ever did for women was to choose Mary Magdalene (the woman at the tomb on Easter morning), to be the first preacher of the good news: "JESUS IS ALIVE!" ("Go tell my disciples, and Peter, that I am risen from the dead.")

Do you think women should preach?

By now you know that I don't think anybody should preach unless called to preach — and if God makes the choice, who should complain?

But understanding the nature of preaching really helps to answer the question. There is a definite difference between an address or a speech, and a sermon. A speech can be an opinion given by a human, perhaps a discussion, an idea, or a theory. A sermon is not (or certainly should not be) the words of man, nor his opinion — it is proclamation. Preaching is a "thus saith the Lord" event. The preacher (male or female) is simply a "channel," a "voice," a "mouthpiece," an "instrument" through which God is heard. As long as this concept is faithfully followed and practiced, then it must be understood that when the Word is proclaimed it is irrelevant whether the vessel used is male or female, but it is imperative that God is heard.

The sermons in this book are printed by requests — other than my own. If they can be a means of blessing, enlightenment, or "instruction in righteousness," they have been given their reason for being.

A woman preach? — it's *your* question, *you* answer it!

Barbara Brokhoff

It's Not So Bad To Be A Beggar . . .

Now Peter and John were going up to the temple at the hour of prayer, the ninth hour. And a man lame from birth was being carried, whom they laid daily at that gate of the temple which is called Beautiful to ask alms of those who entered the temple. Seeing Peter and John about to go into the temple, he asked for alms. And Peter directed his gaze at him, with John, and said, "Look at us." And he fixed his attention upon them, expecting to receive something from them. But Peter said, "I have no silver and gold, but I give you what I have; in the name of Jesus Christ of Nazareth, walk." And he took him by the right hand and raised him up; and immediately his feet and ankles were made strong. And leaping up he stood and walked and entered the temle with them, walking and leaping and praising God. And all the people saw him walking and praising God, and recognized him as the one who sat for alms at the Beautiful Gate of the temple; and they were filled with wonder and amazement at what had happened to him."

— Acts 3:1-10

Nobody wants to be a beggar.

They used to come to our door, when I was a child, and my mother always fed them. They must have had a special language among them, for it seemed to us children that every hungry, needy beggar finally found his way to our house. Mother never turned one away. We were very poor ourselves, and when we would protest her constant kindness to them in giving them a free meal, our mother had a standard reply: "Now children, you know the Bible says 'Inasmuch as ye did it unto the least of these, ye did it unto me' — and you never know when we might be feeding Jesus." Even we couldn't knock the idea of feeding "him" so the beggars continued to be fed. Occasionally we'd comment on the fact that mother always boiled and sterilized the utensils which the beggars ate from, and ask, "If we are feeding Jesus, how come he is dirtier than the rest of us?" (But we didn't ask often, for mother didn't like that kind of sassy talk and, with her black eyes snapping, would soon hush our remarks.)

That's my first recollection of beggars; we've all seen many of them. And now, in this text in Acts, there is a beggar in the narrative with Peter and John. Have you ever noticed how, in reading the Bible stories, we like to relate to the good guys? We readily relate to Joseph the dreamer, but never to his selfish, ugly brothers. We identify with poor, abused Abel, but seldom with sinful Cain. We can imagine ourselves to be a mighty man of faith like Abraham, but can't think we'd ever act like his nephew, Lot. So in this account, we like to take the place of Peter and John in the story, piously intoning on the ears of the beggar: "Such as I have, give I thee", but it never dawns upon us that we are much more likely to be in close kinship with the beggar of the story. Look at it.

Beggars are poor — so are we, nothing we have is ours except it is given to us, even our next breath must come to us from God's mercy.

Beggars are usually dirty — so are we, by nature we are vile, sinful, and unclean.

Beggars are often in rags — so are we, for all our righteousness in God's sight is as filthy rags.

Beggars are often handicapped with sickness — so are we, for the terrible sickness and disease of sin has fastened itself upon us, and we cannot cure it.

Beggars are sometimes blind — so are we, often so blind we cannot even see God when he is closest to us.

Beggars are sometimes lame — as the man in this account — so are we, for man took that fall in the Garden of Eden and has been terribly crippled ever since.

So you see! No doubt about it! We are the beggar in the story. Sounds bad, until you stop to think about it a bit, and then you suddenly realize:

IT'S NOT SO BAD TO BE A BEGGAR
IF YOU GO TO THE RIGHT PLACE.

Just because you are a beggar doesn't mean you have to be stupid. This beggar is really pretty smart. He has found, as any intelligent beggar does, the right place to do his begging. You can beg lots of places.

You can beg on a busy street corner, and people passing by will toss you a coin and tell you to "have a nice day."

You can beg at a large department store, and the customers will put coins in your cup.

You can beg at a school, they'll give you a book, maybe even teach you how to read it.

You can beg at a hospital, they'll give you medication, or even a blood transfusion if you are bleeding to death.

But if you are a really smart beggar, you realize that the church is the best place to beg. This man's "spot" was the gate of the temple. He had learned that the church is the world's best-equipped facility for handling the needs of a beggar! You get more, much more, there than any other spot in town.

The beggar writing this sermon has found the best help I ever received in my life was from the church.

At the church I learned about God — more there than anywhere else.

At the church I learned the memory verses and Bible

stories — without that influence they would probably not be mine today.

At the church I learned about the cross, the sacraments, the creeds.

At the church I learned to pray.

Most of the best experiences of my life have been directly, or at least indirectly, related to the church. Think about it. Isn't that true of you, too?

At the church I learned I was a sinner — but I also learned that Christ died for sinners.

At the church I became a Christian — I was baptizd at the church.

At the church I met my John for the first time — it was in the church we were married.

I've gone to church, so happy that I felt I could not be happier — to find that the church enhanced my joy.

I've gone to church with questions, anxieties, fears, and problems — to find answers, solutions, peace, calm, and direction.

I've returned to church after burying a loved one, broken-hearted with grief — and with tears raining down my face, thought: "I should not have come to church today, I'm not ready" — only to find as I left the church that healing and health had begun and the gaping wound of hurt had had the wondrous balm of Gilead applied and I was getting better.

I announce today that I am hopelessly hooked on the church, totally addicted to it, and if a cure is ever found for this "addiction" I shall refuse it.

I even like "bad" church. By that I mean that I've gone to church, as you have, when the attendance was very low, the choir sang off key, the congregation sang with blasphemous apathy, and the preaching was dull (and we preachers can be dull). My preacher-John says "Some people are so dull they cannot possibly be that way without Divine help," and I have seen preaching so dull it would give an Excedrin a headache! But bad as that kind of church is, and sorry I am that it exists, I would still rather go to that kind of church than to no church at all. I hope I never get over this.

ANY church is beautiful. Don't you love to see them — large cathedrals in the city, modern structures with spires almost erupting from the roof, spotting the countryside with square, brick structures, white frame buildings — all of them beautiful to this beggar's eyes. For the rest of my life I intend to beg at the best gate in the world — the door of the church. No wonder it is called Gate Beautiful.

So you see, it's not so bad to be a beggar if you
GO TO THE RIGHT PLACE —

AT THE RIGHT TIME.

This beggar didn't live at the church. He was brought there each day. The Jews prayed several times a day, and this man was smart enough to be there when the people of God gathered. As beautiful as an empty church may be, it really doesn't do you much practical good until the people of God gather.

It is true that church people are far from being perfect people. but praying people never quite forget what it was like to be a beggar, too. They are people who care. This beggar found that people who go to church to pray and talk to God are also people who will talk to a beggar. He found that people on good terms with God are people who are compassionate and responsive to other's needs. He found out that praying people are giving people — their gratitude is expressed in the grace of giving. They are looking for ways to share what they have.

They are also people who understand. They remember

what it was like before they were "in" the church — when they, too, were outside the gate, crippled, helpless in their sins and sickness. That's why people in the church ought to be the most sympathetic and understanding of all people. That's why it is a tragic indictment against us if we are gossipy, super-critical, and judgmental of others. We must never forget what it was like to be a beggar in sin "outside" the fold of God. Any person needing compassion, understanding, help and rehabilitation ought to find it easier to obtain at the local church than at the local bar. God help us if we ever forget "the pit from which we were digged" — we were brought in — so we must never, never step over, step around, or step on beggars who are still outside.

See! It's not so bad to be a beggar if you are in the
RIGHT PLACE
at the RIGHT TIME,
with
THE RIGHT REQUEST.

Someone has called this the story of "the man who asked for alms and got legs." He really didn't know what to ask for — alms was all beggars ever asked for. They just begged for a coin to buy enough bread to get them through the day, so they could live to beg another day for more bread to live to beg again — and so on for the rest of their lives.

The beggar in the text really got a lot more than he asked for. We, inside the church, often fail to ask for enough. We ask as if we were asking of another beggar, forgetting that our needs are supplied by the King of the Universe.

It is said that Alexander the Great liked to feel his subjects could come to him about any matter. One day a saucy little beggar gained audience with Alexander and asked him for a farm for himself, a new house for his wife, a dowry for his daughter, and an education for his son. Alexander granted the large request, and when he left, the men of his court said, "Why did you let that impudent little fellow have it all, he asked for so much? And Alexander replied; "I liked it, he treated me like a King, he asked big."

We ask of God so pitifully small — when the Word is full of injuctions to bring our requests to a big God. "Ask and ye shall receive;" "Ye have not because ye ask not;" "Ask largely that your joys may be full." God always answers prayer. No prayer ever goes unheard. It is true the answer may be somewhat different from the request (it was for the beggar in this story), but he always answers. He may say, "No" or "Yes" or "Wait" or "I'm going to surprise you " — but he does answer.

Two basic things to remember about prayer are that prayer must always be prayed in and through the name of Jesus, and prayer must always be "if it be thy will."

Could it be God is just waiting for you to ask for more — that you aren't asking enough of him? Did you ever learn the simple little verse which says (it is about a question once posed to a small child):

"If you had been living when Christ was on earth,
    and had met the Saviour kind,
What would you have asked him to do for you — just
    supposing that you were stone-blind?"
The child considered, and then replied, "I expect
    that without a doubt,
I'd have asked for a seeing-eye dog and a collar and
    chain, to lead me daily about."
And how often, thus, in our faithless prayers, we
    acknowledge with shamed surprise,
We have only asked for a dog and a collar and chain,
    when we might have had opened eyes!

Remember, we are asking of a king!

It's not so bad to be a beggar when God sees to it that you always get more than you ask for!

I asked him to forgive my sins, and he did,
    but he not only delivered me from sin and death and hell,
        he gave me also life and heaven!

I keep telling you, it's not so bad to be a beggar if you are in
    THE RIGHT PLACE,
        AT THE RIGHT TIME,
            WITH THE RIGHT REQUEST
                and with
                    THE RIGHT ATTITUDE.

We make it very difficult for God's help to come to us sometimes, because we have such a poor attitude. Note that Peter said: "Look on us" — and the text says the beggar "looked, expecting to receive something."
    See, he looked, expecting . . .
        obedience and faith . . .

Obedience and faith are vital ingredients to getting your needs met. They are so essential that the Bible says "He that cometh to God must believe (see the faith?) that he is, and that he is a rewarder of them that diligently seek him."

We were preaching in Mississippi awhile back and the host pastor came in the parsonage, grinning from ear to ear. He had just called on one of his parishioners, a little lady who, that day, was 103 years old. He said to her: "How did you happen to live so long?" And she replied, "That's easy, preacher, I just trust and obey, drink ice water and crochet!"

Now I'm not so sure about that ice water and crocheting bit, but she was right on dead-center about the trusting and obeying. Those are absolute necessities in cultivating the proper attitude for heaven's help.

And the result of this beggar's being
    IN THE RIGHT PLACE,
        AT THE RIGHT TIME,
            WITH THE RIGHT REQUEST,
                AND THE RIGHT ATTITUDE
was that now the
BEGGAR OUTSIDE IS ANOTHER BEGGAR INSIDE!

Now this is suddenly no ordinary run-of-the-mill prayer meeting that day. There is a marvelous, miraculous healing of this lame man and now he is in the church, walking, leaping, running, shouting, and praising God. (I can't blame him for that, can you?)

The service that day probably didn't have much dignity, but it probably didn't have any apathy either. Propriety is to be desired, but not to the exclusion of expression. Orderly worship services are my personal "choice," but may God help us not to stifle his working among us. Aren't you a little tired of those who never get "turned on" for God? They are excited over a hockey game, a football game, a new car, a raise in pay, their children's accomplishments — but God is so dull to them!

Maybe the cure for some of the indifference in our churches would be to have some "healed beggars inside" — some saved sinners.

The church is full of beggars ... all of us ...
    once we were blind, now we see,
    once we were lame, now we can walk,
    once we were dirty, now we are clean,
    once we were bound, now we are free,

once we were sinnners, now we are saved.

Now it really isn't so bad to be a beggar, is it?

What Gives You Away?

Then said they unto him, "Say now Shibboleth:"
and he siad "Sibboleth," for he could not frame to
pronounce it right."
                                                    — *Judges 12:6*

Not everyone can frame a word the same way — some
words are harder to pronounce than others; almost
everybody has at least one word which gives him trouble
to say. Little children, just learning to speak, often have
trouble making an "l" or an "r." A small boy, in a church I
served as pastor, had this problem. It was a delight to
ask him to say: "I really like to see little rabbits run", for
when he said it, it came out: "I weally wike wo see wittle
wabbits wun."

This Old Testament text has a similar situation. Gilead
and Ephraim are in a great fight, and Ephraim is getting
the worst of the battle, and they decide to head for home.
On their retreat they come to the fords of the Jordan
River. To get home they must get to the other side, but
since there are no bridges, some places are too wide to
swim, others too narrow to wade, they must go to a good
crossing spot. The order has been given to all the
Gileadites to slay any Ephraimite on the spot. Naturally
they go to the crossing places of the river to nab them.
Their problem is that they don't know how to tell the
difference between a man from Ephraim and one of their
own men. They all looked the same, they all dressed the
same — how to tell friend from foe is the dilemma. Then
the Gileadites remembered that the men of Ephraim had
a brogue of their own, making some words distinct from
any of the other tribes. Shibboleth was the word that
stood for river, and so when a man from Ephraim, fleeing
for his life, was apprehended by a man from Gilead he
would be asked: "Friend or foe?" Naturally he would

respond that he was a "friend." Then came the big test: "Then say 'Shibboleth' " — and no matter how hard he tried, no matter how he twisted his tongue, the best the men of Ephraim were able to manage was "Sibboleth" — and they would be killed on the spot.

Such a small difference — the difference between sounding an "h" or not sounding it. Yet, it meant life or death. Not much difference, yet such a small thing gave them away. It is, after all, such small things that give us away as to whether we are Christian or non-Christian. We look the same as most people, we dress the same, live in the same world, often work at the same jobs. What then is to identify us as Christian? What tells on us — what gives us away?

WHAT WE TALK ABOUT GIVES US AWAY

Humans will talk. It is our way of communication. If we have bitterness, it will come out. If we have doubts, they soon will be known. If we are frustrated, others will find out. If we are jealous, it will come to the surface. We talk, verbalize, and discuss issues, people, and all sorts of things — and it is finally our speech that gives us away. You recall that a little maid said to Peter, while he warmed himself by the enemy's fire; "Thy speech betrayeth thee." Maybe that's why the wisdom of one of the Proverbs says: "Even a fool is thought wise when he keeps silent."

We talk about all sorts of things — both the Christian and the non-Christian. There is no difference in the fact that we all talk. But there should be a difference in what we talk about.

It is very easy to be guilty of speaking a lot — but only of trivia, of incidentals, non-essentials. We saturate conversation with nothings and "small talk" such as "the weather," "Green Stamps versus Eagle Stamps," the number of calories in a slice of bread, soap opera events, and other "major" matters of minor importance.

There was a man who sought a divorce. He told the judge his wife was driving him crazy, that she talked all the time. "She never stops talking," he complained. "What does she talk about?" inquired the judge. The man replied, "You see, that's just it, your honor, she ain't said nothin' yet!"

Sometimes when we talk it is not just "nothings" — it is worse. It is gossipy, critical, judgmental, and condescending to others. Sometimes it is grumbling and complaining. This is not a minor offense for a Christian. It can spoil the whole climate of your life. It takes the joy out of service to God and others, it destroys unity and fellowship. It is a plague to the church. If a fellow Christian is at fault, we are not supposed to gossip and sit in judgment, we are to pray for him. Paul wrote: "Brethren, if a man be overtaken in a fault, ye which are spiritual, restore such an one in the spirit of meekness, considering thyself, lest thou also be tempted."

Then, there are a few persons who realize that the things they talk about do influence others, so they decide to talk about the church, and about God but they do it in such awkward ways. They are embarrassed, or apologetic — doing it out of a sense of "duty" or a responsibility to "witness" to their faith — and what they say is forced, artificial, and unconvincing.

Then there are those great souls who just simply cannot *not* talk about him. Jesus Christ is very real to them, they love him, they love his church, so that speaking of him is as natural for them as breathing. They are like the disciples who said, having been commanded to speak or preach no more in Jesus' name: "We cannot but speak the things we have seen and heard." Their spontaneity, naturalness, and ease of conversation is like a warm, refreshing breeze in a room of stagnant air.

Would it not be great if our tongues could be as dedicated as was the tongue of Jesus? It was said of him "Never man spake like this man." He spoke words of tenderness, "Come unto me and I will give you rest;" words of peace, "Peace I leave with you, my peace I give unto you;" words of hope, "In my Father's house are many mansions, I go to prepare a place for you;" words of forgiveness, "Father, forgive them" — each time Jesus spoke, people saw God. Whom do others see when you speak?

God tells us, through the prophet Malachi, about a special book he has in which are recorded the names of those who love him and speak often of him — here on earth. "Then they that loved the Lord spoke often one to another, and a book of remembrance shall be written of them, and they shall be mine in that day when I make up my jewels, saith the Lord." Other than having your name inscribed in the Book of Life, can you think of any other better place than to have your name in this Book of Remembrance? It comes of loving him much and speaking often of him to one another.

You see, what you talk about really does give you away.

Does your tongue say "Shibboleth" or "Sibboleth"?

WHATEVER IS MOST IMPORTANT TO US GIVES US AWAY

What are the priorities of your life? They will give you away every time!

Some people have as the goal of their life to make money; others are consumed with establishing a good reputation;

some concentrate on fun and good times;
for others it is success in business;
it can be your family, money, children, sex, golf,
or anything.
Your priority may be God — but remember this,
no matter what you say,
WHATEVER IS FIRST IN YOUR LIFE
IS REALLY YOUR GOD.

When things are more important to us then people we are in trouble, when people are more important than God, we are still in trouble.

Oddly enough, you never have to announce to anyone what your priorities are. Anyone who knows you at all already knows what is most important to you. No matter what you say, your children, your family, your friends all know if your business, your family, your church, or anything else is ahead of God in your life. You give yourself away.

A beautiful, true story is told of an incident in the life of Billy Sunday, the flaming evangelist of another generation. He met a man in one of his meetings, liked the man, found him to be a truly dedicated Christian, and some months later wanted to contact him, only to realize he had forgotten the man's name. Billy Sunday remembered only the place from which he had come. So Billy Sunday addressed a letter to him, and the envelope read only: "God's Man, Adrian, Michigan." When the postmaster in Adrian, Michigan read it, he knew exactly which box to put it in! Let me ask "If a letter should come to your postman, addressed simply: "God's Man (or Woman), the name of your town, state, and zip code, would it occur to your postman to put the letter in your box?

This illustration is another way of asking:
Do your priorities say "Shibboleth" or "Siboleth?"

OUR UNCONSCIOUS REACTIONS GIVE US A WAY

The late E. Stanley Jones says that there is "such a thing as having such a sound experience of conversion to Jesus Christ that even your unconscious reactions are converted." By "unconscious reactions" we mean those automatic, unthinking, unpremeditated actions. If these are to be good reactions, it must be impelled from within. Only the truly redemptive force of the Holy Spirit can do this for us. Without his power we blow our tops, become quickly and easily angry, frustrated, upset, and nervous. It is not that we ever intend to be un-Christian, it is just that we are inadequate of ourselves to be or do differently.

Most Christians don't worry a lot about committing large, glaring, external sins such as robbing banks, committing adultery, killing someone, or stealing another's property. But you might have trouble reacting as you should inwardly when everyday experiences of life pile up on you. You might unconsciously, and without thinking, react in bad temper, with envy, jealousy, self-pity, anger, spite, hatefulness, or swearing.

I came upon a scene in a church I served as pastor. Just as I opened a door where the men were working at redecorating the fellowship hall, one of the men hit the wrong nail (his thumb) with a hammer. He immediately reacted by saying, "Damn, damn, damn, damn," (and quite a few other expletives which I have deleted) — and then seeing me quickly and repentantly said: "O preacher, please excuse me, it just happend so fast it came out before I had time to think." I can understand that, can't you? Haven't you reacted at times in a manner that, had you had time to think it through, you would have said or done things differently?

One man said to another, as they contemplated some evil they wanted to do to a third man. "There is no use bothering him, every time you cut him all he does is bleed love."

Don't you want to ask God to let your knowledge of him so permeate all of you, that even your unconscious reactions will be Christian? What do they say now of you — "Shibboleth" or "Sibboleth?"

HOW DO YOU SAY IT?

Well, what gives you away?
    Does your whole life say "Shibboleth" or "Sibboleth?"
        It's another way of asking, "Does your life say "JESUS"?
Or does it come out sounding like something else?

How To Be A Saint In A Storm

I now bid you take heart; for there will be no loss of life among you, but only of the ship. For this very night there stood by me an angel of the God to whom I belong and whom I worship, and he said, "Do not be afraid, Paul; you must stand before Caesar; and lo, God has granted you all those who sail with you." So take heart, men, for I have faith in God that it will be exactly as I have been told.

— Acts 27:22-25

How do you act in a storm?

A friend, who is terribly afraid to fly, was invited to speak at a special gathering of the religious body of which he was a part, in Frankfurt, Germany. As he approached the airport in New York a terrific storm was taking place. He dreaded the trip, and now that the storm increased in velocity, he was sure that the flight would be cancelled. He continued to think this, even as he approached the ticket desk, and finally was ushered aboard his plane. He began to think seriously about the flight when they revved up the engines and taxied out to the end of the runway. He kept desperately hoping for a last-minute cancellation of the flight — surely someone would notice this weather is too bad to fly in — and was about to be reassured when he heard the voice of a man coming over the intercom system of the plane. "Now," he thought, "they are going to announce that we can't fly after all." But the voice of the man was saying: "Ladies and gentlemen, your attention, please! Ladies and gentlemen, this is your captain." (and my friend began to relax in anticipation of the flight cancellation, at last). "Ladies and gentlemen, may I have your attention for this announcement? This is your captian. This pilot and co-pilot will be flying you overseas in a 747 jet — we will be flying non-stop to Frankfurt, Germany — we will be flying at a speed of about 650 miles per hour — we will be flying at an altitude of approximately 35,000 feet — we will take off just as soon as I get up nerve enough!" My friend was in a panic, unfastening his seat-belt, and preparing for instantly leaving the plane — only to realize they were now airborne! He said, "So I prayed, Oh, how I prayed! There was nothing left to do but pray!"

We all react differently in life's crises, in the storms and stress that come to each of us. Some of us try to run, others pray, some have hysterics, some give up in despair, others face the battle head-on. In the chapter of the text we have the example of one of God's great men showing us how to react as Christians in a crisis, how to be a saint in a storm.

The scene opens with a conference aboard the ship. There are nearly 300 men on this ship, but the conference seems to involve only four of them: Julius, who represents the military power of Rome — the man in charge of the prisoners on board. Then there is the owner of the ship, possibly the man who also owns most of the cargo — representative of capital. The third man is the captain of the boat, the man of the sea. Finally, there is Paul, a preacher and a prisoner.

They are trying to decide: shall we stay in the Port called by the deceptively nice sounding name, Fair Havens — and maybe be stuck here all winter — or shall we try to make Phoenix, a better port, and more commodious harbor?

Julius wants to sail, the owner feels they should sail, the captain is willing to sail — only Paul feels they should go no farther. But he is out-voted by the others (after all, what does a preacher-prisoner know?) who feel they can somehow make a better port in which to spend the winter.

So, they set sail on a day when the south wind is blowing softly — what a great day for sailing!

But winds change, and this one suddenly shifts direction, and the delightful sailing breeze is now a "northeaster" blowing upon them in terrifying fury! It's interesting to note that the Bible (KJV) says the name of the storm was Euroclydon. I keep telling you the Bible is more up-to-date than tomorrow's newspaper! Did you think the American Meteoroligical Association was the first to think up the gimmick of giving names to hurricanes ... like Agnes, Bertha, Camille, Delia, etc? See, the Bible did it first!

And this storm is no summer squall that is over in about thirty minutes. In fact it rages for hours, then a day, two days, seven days, ten days, and at the end of two weeks they are still in the middle of a storm that won't quit!

The situation aboard ship is hopeless. The men are ready to give up in despair. They are sure death is near. They haven't seen sun or moon or stars in many days (and no 20th century navigational equipment either), they don't know where they are, where they've been, or where they are going. See them huddled together on the deck, in the hold of the ship — anxious, fearful, terrified, waiting for the end to come.

However bad your imagination lets you see it — it's worse than that!
It's a darker time than anyone has ever encountered —
and in the middle of that kind of hopeless situation,
the preacher stands up among them and says:
"BE OF GOOD CHEER!"

Now here is a man who is either completely bereft of his senses, or else he has the most fantastic faith you've ever seen. This is good news born of great confidence in God, or else the raving of a blithering idiot.

"Be of good cheer!" — in this kind of situation?

If you are going to do anything then (or now in our world), and have a message like this, you'd better have something pretty good to back it up with.

Upon what basis is Paul able to say these words?

No need telling them the boat is a "good old boat" and will surely stand the storm, they can already see it is about to fall apart. He doesn't tell them they have some pretty important people on board, so everything will be fine — everyone can see they are as scared as anybody. No use telling them the captain is very skilled, a real "man of the sea" — they know that, but they know he's lost too. No point in saying he just got the latest "weather report" and it's going to be "clearing" tomorrow.

No, that kind of optimism is no good. That which denies the obvious never helps anyone.

The easy mouthings of adages, when we are in a storm or crisis, doesn't do much good. Platitudes and pious sayings carry little weight in real trouble.

How about those "easy" words, when life falls in upon you, of those who say: "Cheer up, it will all come out in the wash" (and you weren't planning on washing it anyhow) — or — "It will be all right; a hundred years from now you won't know the difference" (enough to make you mad enough to fight, isn't it?)

If you are going to mouth words of cheer and encouragement you must have sound reason for it — and Paul has!

He said: Be of good cheer —
for there stood by me this night the angel of God, whose I am and whom I serve, and he promised me not only my life, but the lives of all who sail with me, so Cheer up, for I believe God.

How's that for a ringing, confident faith? "I believe God!"

This is the kind of conviction that speaks to us in our deepest needs. The world is dying all about us for a contact with persons who are on recent, intimate, speaking terms with God and who believe him!

(No wonder Billy Graham gets so many letters,
no wonder Oral Roberts gets so many prayer requests,
no wonder so many religious "fanatics" are consulted —
people are desperately seeking someone, anyone who is in
direct contact with God who has a word of hope for them in
their situation.)

This is what faith does for the saint in a storm, it gives an unshakable confidence in God. It believes in the midst of the storm (not after the storm has passed by and the tumult subsides). Faith believes when it can't see. The way of the unbeliever is "Seeing is believing" — it is just the oppostie for the person of faith: "Believing is seeing."

But while faith has a strong confidence, in the supernatural, it doesn't sit around and wait for God to do for us what we can do for ourselves. You'll recall that when God gave Peter the miraculous deliverance from prison by sending his Earthquake Angel, the angel opened the doors, opened the iron gate, the angel struck off his chains — but the angel told Peter he could put on his own cloak and sandals. God expects you to do what you can do.

Now this is the way faith and confidence in God always works. It believes absolutely in the divine help that God can and will give, but there is another side to the coin. There is also the PRACTICAL SIDE. And God blesses the action of the saint as surely as he blesses his faith. So now, having encouraged them with a "word from God," Paul gives some very sensible, practical advice.

He begins by telling them they must

STAY WITH THE SHIP.

Some of the crew want to embark on their own, save themselves, forget what happens to the others. Paul reminds them they must stay together. Faith is always a uniting and cohesive force, never a divisive one.

And it is still true — in our churches today we need everybody. True, some are hard to get along with, cantankerous, unfaithful, stingy, apathetic, selfish, and even downright ornery — but the church needs them all. Our world must be held together by our common faith in God or it cannot be saved.

You want to watch anyone, no matter how "religious" or "holy" or "spiritually deep" they may be, when their words or actions would cause schism in the body of Christ. The Holy Spirit calls, enlightens, and gathers, and that which splits, divides, and polarizes is not of faith.

Then Paul further suggests: "Let down your anchors and wait for the day."

STABILIZE THE SITUATION

It does seem rather obvious, doesn't it? Since it is dark, we can't navigate by sun, moon, or stars; we may be drifting farther and farther from our destination, we may be nearing reefs and rocks — let's be practical, sensible, put down our anchors and wait for the day. Maybe we'll be able to see something and more advisedly assess our situation. Common sense, isn't it? Certainly the example suggests to us a stabilizing, a grounding, a security.

Every Christian needs to put his faith in something solid. What are the anchors for your life when the crisis comes? Do you have any absolutes that hold when the storms begin to blow every direction? Every Christian needs to sit down and sort out what he actually believes for sure relative to his faith. Let me illustrate. I don't have too many absolutes, things for which I'd stake my life — and yours might not have to be the same as mine — but I could not attempt to live a life of faith without something to hold on to as an anchor. Let me name four of mine.
1. I believe in God (not everyone does, you know).
2. I believe that Jesus is the Divine Son of God, and my Savior.
3. I believe that the Bible is the Word of God.
4. I believe I am called to preach.

I'm not sure I could handle the stress of life's storms without these certainties. Do you have any absolutes that you claim as your own?

Then, you can't get much more practical than Paul's next move —

HE FED THEM

"You're going to need your strength — so get some food in you."

All some Christians need to improve their faith is a good meal and/or a good night's sleep. Some of the time, when your faith is low, it may well be that your body is depleted of food or rest. Nine hundred-calorie-a-day diets can even make some people mean. Faith gets at a low ebb when the body needs physical attention. Let me cite a biblical example.

Remember the great prophet of God, Elijah, who called down fire from God out of heaven? His prayer of about sixty-six words was answered by God who sent fire upon a sacrifice that had been doused with twelve barrels of water! Elijah has such mighty faith in God to do such impossible things! And yet, after such ultimate triumph on Mt. Carmel, a few hours later when Queen Jezebel threatens his life, he runs a full day's journey into the wilderness, falls down under a tree, feels very low and sorry for himself, and asks God to let him die! He didn't really want to die — if he did he could have stayed where he was and Jezebel would have handled it for him easily.

How can a man of such remarkable faith fall into such despair? How can such a threat bother him in the face of the larger battles he has already won? What great, staggering, profound solution will God offer to his prophet?
> God lets him sleep.
>> Lets him sleep and rest, and when he wakes up, he feeds him . . . God feeds him some angel-food cake

(I'm sure it was angel-food cake, it was cake brought by an angel, wasn't it? I can't in my wildest imaginings think it was devil's-food cake, can you?) And when the weary, hungry prophet is rested and fed, he is able to again hear the still small voice of God and to be the prophet of power that God had called him to be.

A practical move may not look so great always, but it

may well be at times the "saintliest" thing you can do in that moment.

And Paul encourages them to

NEVER STOP DOING WHAT YOU CAN!

They are still working with the ship in the storm and decide to "lighten the ship" by throwing the wheat overboard. It may not help, but at least it's worth a try. This example seems to say to us that we must always do, however small it seems to be, what we can. The Christophers have a motto which says: "It is better to light one small candle than to curse the darkness."

THEN, WATCH GOD BE TRUE TO HIS WORD!

After you've brought your faith into action,
    after you've done all that seems realistic and practical,
        what's the next step of the saint in a storm?

Then you watch God be true to himself and his Word. When the chapter ends — the roll is called, they are all drying themselves by a fire on the shore, they are all there. Just like that preacher said, "no lives lost" — "all saved."

Sounds like the ending of a fairy tale — "they all lived happily ever after." We never need to worry about God's keeping his end of the bargain, we just need to check ourselves to see if we are doing all we should.

So now you are on your way to becoming a saint in the storms of life, but you do this by being a saint first when there is no storm. The late Bishop Arthur James Moore says you don't become a saint suddenly: "You become what you have been being for a long time."

Are you a saint in a storm? Do you act like a Christian in a crisis?

At least Paul, the man of God, has shown us now how it's done.

God Made Me Do It!

*So Joseph said to his brothers, "Come near to me,
I pray you." And they came near. And he said, "I
am your brother, Joseph, whom you sold into
Egypt. And now do not be distressed, or angry
with yourselves, because you sold me here; for
God sent me before you to preserve life. For the
famine has been in the land these two years; and
there are yet five years in which there will be
neither plowing nor harvest. And God sent me
before you to preserve for you a remnant on
earth, and to keep alive for you many survivors.
So it was not you who sent me here, but God."*
— *Genesis 45:4-8a*
[*Context from Genesis, chapters 37-48*]

"God sent me", "God made me" — strange words for
most people to say! We say instead, "The devil made me
do it!" It is almost remarkable then, that in a few short
verses in the text, Joseph says four times: "God sent
me," "God made me."

Joseph feels that all of his life is under the guiding hand
of God. Since God is his master, Joseph feels that no
matter what happens — of good or bad — sadness or joy
— God is in it and nothing can touch him but that God
will ultimately work it out for the best.

Things did not always go easily and well for Joseph. He
was sold into slavery in Egypt by jealous brothers. He
was as good as dead as far as they were concerned. He
wound up in charge of things at Potiphar's house, and
then was unjustly imprisoned because of Potiphar's wife.
He was in prison for two years, and while there the
governor of the prison put him in charge of the other
prisoners. There he interpreted dreams for a butler and
a baker — and waited two long years for the butler to

remember the favor he did for him. Finally, in a long series of events, he was made second-in-command in Pharaoh's court, and while he is working by Pharaoh's side he not only saved enough corn to feed all of Egypt, but to feed the children of Israel who came to buy from him. Now, in the text, the murderous brothers of Joseph stood before him, and he spoke in words that remind us just how high hope can go and still not be dashed to pieces. He said to them: "Don't be angry with yourselves — God did it — God sent me before you to preserve life. You did not send me here, but God did it!"

Joseph's words do not mean that God actually willed the treacherous deed of his brothers any more than God incited the stoning of Stephen or the imprisonment of John Bunyon. What it does mean is that God used Stephen's stoning as a factor in Paul's conversion, and used Bunyon's jail as a chance to inspire and give to the world *Pilgrim's Progress.*

Crimes are done to us and others and God does not will it, but the insight of faith sees that while God may permit evil in our dark world (he has to take that risk if we are to have freedom of will), faith still knows that when evil takes the game of life into its own hands, God is still Master of the situation. This is the gospel truth (or there is no gospel for our lives at all) that in proportion as I yield myself to the will of God — the same power that turned Christ's death into victory will do the same for me.

This confidence means that difficulties will be transformed, trials will have meaning, joys will be enhanced, sins be forgiven, and even in death I shall have everlasting life.

That's what Joseph had in mind when he talked about God leading him! That is what the God-directed life is all about. Most of us have never become serious about this matter of letting God lead us in *ALL* of life. We were glad to learn that Jesus will be our Savior, for we know we are sinners and need his forgiveness — but it is quite another thing for God to have all our moments and all our days and direct us in everything.

Letting Jesus be *Savior* is one thing, but
letting Jesus be *Lord* is another matter.

Consider what might happen if we decided to really live God-directed lives, as Joseph did.

THE GOD-DIRECTED LIFE —

DOESN'T MEAN YOU WON'T BE MISUNDERSTOOD

Joseph's brothers never did like him very much. They were jealous of him because of his father's partiality, because he was the owner of that long-sleeved coat of many colors, because of his ambitious dreams. Come to think of it, his ever-loving father wasn't too happy about some of his dreams.

Now, in living the God-lead, God-ordered life, you are living in some kind of a fool's paradise if you think just because you are a Christian that everything will always be sweetness and light. You may as well know right now that you won't be able to please everybody. Some people will understand you and your works and your actions, others will not. Some will take your deeds and misconstrue them any way but the way you meant them. People don't understand us, often because they don't want to, but many times because we don't make ourselves clear, or assume too much.

My good and dear friend, Peg Cromartie, tells a delightful story of a teacher-friend of hers who teaches the third grade. Many of the children are underprivileged, but all of them delightful. One little black boy who had grown to love his teacher, and wanted to do something for her, brought her a leaf to school one day. The teacher immediately sensed that it was a special gift, so she said: "O I just love it. I'll take it home and put it in water. My mother has a green thumb, and I just know it will grow!" The teacher resumed her duties, the boy went back to his desk, but in a few minutes was waving his hand wildly in the air for attention, and saying: "Teacher, teacher, I want to ast you somethin' " "All right," she said, "What is it?" "It's about your mother, teacher. Teacher, if her thumb is green, what color is the other fingers?"

Right at the beginning of living the God-directed life you need to know that sometimes you will not be clear in what you say, someone will question your motives, wrong interpretations be given to what you say . . . you can't please everyone. Some people will not understand you, others will not like you, some will not give you the benefit of the doubt, and not everyone will think you are great.

But why should we think that is strange? Jesus Christ, the perfect, sinless, holy, good, and divine Son of God had people who misunderstood him too — how can we ever presume to think we can be above our Lord and live without the same problem?

THE GOD-DIRECTED LIFE —

DOESN'T MEAN YOU WON'T BE TEMPTED

Look how Joseph must have been tempted.

It must have been quite a temptation to take Potiphar's wife while no one was looking. After all, he is a long way from home — it won't hurt his father's good name, besides all the other slaves in Egypt do that sort of thing. Besides, his master trusts him and he could get by with it. Add to that the fact that no one will ever know — the woman is willing — she is seductive, probably very beautiful — quite a temptation!

Or how about the butler. Joseph did him a favor — and had to stay in prison two long years just because this man forgot all about him . . . what a temptation to now say: "I remember how you treated me, I'll have your head for that!"

And what about his brothers? Think of *that* temptation! They stand before him now. They one time planned to kill him, sold him instead in order to make a dollar profit from him. Now Joseph has them in his power . . . his brothers can be made to suffer, to really pay for what they did to him!

Temptation takes many forms yet today. It's always tempting to take revenge on those who wrong us. Revenge "feels good," is "sweet." A dentist friend tells of a small boy who came into his office for treatment for a baby tooth. The lad was about six years of age. The tooth had been hurting the child every time he ate candy, or cake, or ice cream, or anything sweet. The dentist took a look at the tooth and decided to end the boy's problem once-for-all, so he just quickly pulled it — threw it into the waste basket, and told the boy to go home and feel good again. But the lad, before leaving the office, walked over to the waste basket, rummaged around in it until he found his tooth, stuck it in his blue-jeans pocket, and started to leave. The dentist said: "I bet I know what you are going to do with that. You are going to take it home and put it under your pillow and let the tooth-fairy find it." "Oh, no, I'm not," the boy replied, "I'm going to take it home, sprinkle sugar on it, and watch it hurt!"

Let me remind you again that living the God-directed life
doesn't mean you'll never be tempted again. Tempted to
sin, to take revenge, to stray, to retaliate. Temptation
takes so many forms — and is always so logical. When
the devil tempted Jesus in the wilderness, after fasting
for forty days, the temptation was not to make him a
seven course meal, or even cake, just bread. What harm
could there possibly be in a piece of bread?

THE GOD-DIRECTED LIFE —

DOESN'T MEAN YOU WON'T BE UNJUSTLY AND UNFAIRLY TREATED

Joseph is put into prison because he *resisted* temptation
— he is punished for a crime he did not commit. That
certainly doesn't seem very fair, does it? Potiphar trusts
him with all that is in his house, including his wife,
Joseph is true to that trust, and then because of the
anger of a proud, spiteful, spurned woman he is thrown
into the Round Tower Prison. Where's the justice in
that?

Can't you just hear what we would say? "Oh, God, what
have I ever done to deserve this?" "Why, me, God, why
me, why?"

We don't like to be punished when we do wrong even
when we are guilty. We really object when we feel
self-righteous and abused and innocent. But we may as
well face it. That's the way life is, even the God-directed
life sometimes.

What can we expect? It also happened to Jesus, the New
Testament Joseph. Jesus came to teach us and we would
have none of his teachings, he came to love us and we
hated him in return, he came to offer us life, and we
killed him!

THE GOD-DIRECTED LIFE —

DOESN'T MEAN YOU WON'T FEEL FORGOTTEN

The butler forgot the favor Joseph had done for him in prison.

Potiphar forgot how faithful and true he had been.

His brothers forgot he was a brother.

Joseph was forgotten for a long time. In fact, it was not until two years later that Pharaoh had a dream and the whole thing began to work out.

Have you noticed how willing we are to let God direct our lives so long as we can set the schedule, so long as he does things in the time we allot him? We say: "God, this is my need. I need it by Tuesday noon. Amen." Then, if we don't have what we've ordered by Tuesday noon we stop believing in Divine Guidance!

But remember:

Joseph waited for two years.

John Bunyon languished in Bedford jail for twelve years.

Monica prayed for that sinful, licentious, profligate son of hers with tears and prayers and moanings and beseechings for thirty-two years before God made him the saint that we call Augustine.

But we are in such a hurry, and we demand that if God is to lead our lives it is by our schedules. We keep forgetting that it is the director and not the directed who keeps the calendar.

Besides, you need never fear that God has failed you, or forgotten you, for he never forgets his own. You are always on his mind and heart.

THE GOD-DIRECTED LIFE —

WHAT GOOD IS IT?

By now, you can see that life deals out experiences with the God-directed life much the same as the one who lets self or the devil direct him.

So, if the Christian is not going to get any special favors,

if you are still going to have troubles in life,

if God is not going to build a special protective wall about you,

if you have some of the same problems everybody else has,

what's the use anyway?

Why bother to let Christ be Lord of all of life?

Never fear, *there is a difference!* The God-directed life absolutely cannot lose. God is ordering your existence,

you never walk alone,

life is like living out a fairy tale ("and they all lived happily ever after"),

the quality of your life is different,

the direction of your life is different,

the ultimate outcome is sure,

and you are always, in time, a winner and not a loser, for

The Lord of Life is in charge!

This is great, glad, grand news, then — it means that in the

GOD-DIRECTED LIFE YOU CAN BE

RESOURCEFUL.

Joseph wanted to live in his own land, but failing to do that he'd enjoy living in Egypt. He wanted to be free, but since he had to be a slave he'd be the best slave Potiphar ever had. He wanted to keep his position there, but if he had to go to prison, he'd be the best prisoner the Round Tower Prison ever had known. He wanted to dream dreams at home, but instead he would interpret them for a butler, a baker, or even a king.

In other words, since Joseph believed God was leading all of life for him, he would use the situation he was in to the best purpose.

Remember learning the poem years ago:
"If you can't be a pine on the top of the hill,
Be a scrub in the valley, but be,
The best little scrub on the side of the hill,
Be a bush, if you can't be a tree."

The Christian, under the direction of God is always doing something. If he can't do one thing, he'd do another, but he will do something. He is not content to do nothing. "Whatever your hand finds to do, do with all your might."

IN THE GOD-DIRECTED LIFE YOU CAN BE

CLEVER AND WISE.

Joseph did not reveal himself to his brothers until the proper time. He very cleverly put his silver cup in Benjamin's bag so he could finally get a true picture of the kind of men his brothers had become — then he'd know how to deal with them. He used his head, as well as his heart, in handling this sticky situation.

Why do we think, just because we are Christians, that we have to put our brains in cold storage? Jesus accused his generation of slowness and stupidity. He said: "The children of this world are wiser than children of light." Another time we are enjoined: "Be wise as serpents and harmless as doves" (we manage to be harmless enough, but not always very wise).

We could use a little wisdom in the work of the Kingdom today. With some of the reporting we do for God and the church, it is no wonder the people stay away in droves. When will we learn to sort out what to say to the non-Christian, to the non-churched? Do you have to tell every weakness, every mistake, every problem that we have? Some of our "reporting" could be of a little wiser caliber, and still be truthful.

Cultivate some Christian tact. A famous preacher once boarded a train to make a trip. When he entered the car, he sat down by a man who had already had too much to drink. The man had tucked under his seat a bottle, concealed in a brown paper bag. Every now and then he would take a drink from the bottle, but always, before drinking, he would offer the bottle to the minister. As time passed, the minister again and again politely refused the offer of a drink, and finally the inebriate said: "What do yo do for a living?" The minister responded, "I'm a preacher." "Oh," said the drunk, "you must think I'm a terrible man!" "No, not at all," said the minister, "It was just going through my mind what a generous man you are!" (Wasn't that better than a hell-fire-and-brimstone indictment on drunkeness?)

If God is directing your life, don't stymie him at every corner. Give him enough cooperation that he doesn't have to spend all his time correcting our stupidities!
THE GOD-DIRECTED LIFE WILL MAKE YOU

TRUSTWORTHY AND USEFUL.

Joseph just could not believe, in prison, that an enraged female was directing his life — so believing that God was still in control, he became the most valuable person around there.

Joseph could not believe that his selfish, wicked brothers held the plans for his life, so he did the best he could for them and for the King of Egypt.

Wherever he was, he had integrity, strength of character, and they found he was honest and could be trusted. And useful? It turned out that he was the most important and useful person around — all because God talked to him, directed him, and led him.

The result? He saved the lives of his father, brothers, and seventy other members of his family;
He saved all of Egypt, and
He saved himself as well!

This text is saturated with Joseph's confidence in God: — "Don't be angry with yourselves"; "You meant it for evil, but God meant it for good"; "You didn't send me here, God did!"

IT WORKED FOR JESUS TOO

We will not always know why our lives turn as they do, the paths they take, why questions remain unanswered. But we will know that God will always come to us and that he is enough for any situation.

Even Christ in Gethsemane had to drink the bitter cup, though he prayed till the blood came, the cross did not go away. In fact, the cross killed him — they even buried him —
but three days later he got resurrection for himself and
for all who believe in him!

The God-Directed Life won't work in parts, in pieces, by halves — some days and not others — it must be a commitment for every day for all of life.
And then it works,
it really works.
Just ask Joseph,
or Jesus,
or try it yourself!

The Most Misunderstood Gift

*"And they were all filled with the Holy Ghost, and
began to speak with other tongues . . .*
—Acts 2:4

There is no doubt — the most misunderstood God of the
Trinity is the Holy Spirit. There is also no doubt — the
most misunderstood gift of the Holy Spirit is the gift of
speaking in tongues. Nearly every Christian has already
chosen his "side" regarding the speaking in tongues. Few
people are neutral on the subject — most are either
"anti-tongues" or "pro-tongues."

Not everybody even wants to hear the pros and cons.
They remind you of the woman who said to her husband,
during a discussion: "Don't confuse me with the facts —
I've already made up my mind."

Those who are *AGAINST* speaking in tongues quote
Paul when he said: "I would rather speak five words with
my understanding, than 10,000 words in an unknown
tongue."

But, strangely enough, those who are *FOR* speaking in
tongues quote Paul also, same book of I Corinthians,
same 14th chapter, one verse away from the other: "I
thank my God I speak in tongues more than ye all!"

It is sad, pathetic, tragic, and true that the subject of
tongues-speaking has become one of the most divisive
topics in the church today. But as Christians, we've got
to listen to reason, to logic, and certainly to what the
Scriptures say, and find biblical truth for our position.
We usually get so carried away with our own dogmatic
stance that we won't have an open mind to hear any
other side than our own.

54

We are often like the woman who heard the great and learned philosopher-psychologist William James deliver a lecture on the solar system. She approached him, at the lecture's conclusion, by saying she had a theory that was far superior to his. She continued: "We don't live on a ball rotating around the sun, as you claim, but we live on a crust of earth on the back of a giant turtle."

The great man decided to dissuade his opponent as gently as possible, so he said: "If your theory is correct, madam, just what does the turtle stand on?"

"You're a very clever man, Mr. James," she replied, "and that's a good question, but I'm ready for you. I can answer it. The first turtle stands on the back of a second, far-larger turtle."

"But," said Mr. James, ever so patiently, "what does the second turtle stand on?" The old woman crowed triumphantly, and said, "It's no use, Mr. James, it's turtles all the way down!"

So, rather than having a closed mind, rather than run the risk of being mistaken — let's look at what the Bible has to say. Of course the Holy Spirit and his work is mentioned all through the Word of God, both in the Old and New Testaments, but most of the teaching we have on speaking in tongues is given to us by Luke in Acts, and by Paul in Corinthians and in Romans.

Perhaps the best approach is to simply provide biblical answers for the questions that most often arise when the subject of tongues is discussed.

IS SPEAKING IN TONGUES
A VALID GIFT AND EXPERIENCE?

Is speaking in tongues a valid gift and experience, or do you have to be some kind of a religious "nut" to practice and participate? No less a Christian than Bishop Fulton Sheen said: "We don't communicate at the academic level anymore, but at the emotional level." (Note that he did not say emotional*ism*, but emotion.)

Speaking in tongues is an experience of the emotions, rather than of the mind and intellect. But to speak in tongues does not mean you have "parked your mind." It does not mean you are following only your feelings, that you are now anti-church, anti-rational, or anti-intellectual. It is a valid gift and experience.

There are three certain, different, definite times recorded in Acts when speaking in tongues occurred. Our text states that on the day of Pentecost they were all filled with the Holy Ghost and began to speak in other tongues. It also occurred in Caesarea and again at Ephesus. Of course we also know that the church at Corinth spoke in tongues, for at least chapters 12, 13, and 14 of 1 Corinthians were written to correct errors in the usage of the gift.

Historically we know that the practice of speaking in tongues occurred in certain churches during the first two and a half centuries of the Christian era. Then, we know little or nothing of its having been a general practice in the church for nearly fourteen centuries — until about 1650 — and then recurred at intervals from that time until 1900 when it began to manifest itself more extensively than ever before. What we know as the Pentecostal movement began about 1900 — and in the last 15 or 20 years we have the neo-Pentecostal (new Pentecostal) movement. This group is best known by its name "charismatic." This tongues movement has gained attention in nearly every mainline Protestant denomination as well as in the Roman Catholic Church.

We Methodists have felt that our stance should say that "we should be open and accepting of those whose Christian experience differs from our own." Since so many people have obviously experienced in truth and in reality the gift of tongues, we have felt the need to look at the gift with openness. We can't say: "Well, I've never spoken in tongues, therefore it is no good!" — nor should we say: "Well, we have never done it before, so why should we start now?" Examination of our ideas and motives makes us realize we often fail to be very logical. Preserving the status-quo experience is no more realistic than Harry Emerson Fosdick's delightful little quatrain he learned as a child:

"I eat my peas with honey — I've done it all my life;
It makes the peas taste funny — but it keeps them on my knife!"

We must not say, "Well, I've never done it, so it's not for me."

That kind of illogic is akin to that of the two small girls who were playing together one afternoon in the park. "I wonder what time it is?" said one of them.

"Well, I don't know, but it can't be four o'clock yet," replied the other with magnificent delusion, "because my mother said I was to be home at four, and I'm not." So, because it is biblical, the New Testament Church practiced it, the early Church experienced it, the Pentecostals of the 1900s and some charismatics of our present day speak in tongues — we must recognize it as a legitimate gift and experience to speak in tongues.

CAN YOU BE FILLED WITH THE HOLY SPIRIT WITHOUT SPEAKING IN TONGUES?

Some proponents of the tongues movement insist that the only valid, sure sign of the Holy Spirit's filling our lives is to speak in unknown tongues. This is false. No where does the New Testament teach this.

If we are to make a good judgment as to the evidence of the Holy Spirit's presence in our lives, it would be to test our love quotient. Love (which, by the way, is one of the fruits of the Spirit) is one of the best evidences whereby we know if the Holy Spirit is truly within us.

The stance of our United Methodist Church in this matter is that we are "critical of classic pentecostalism when it infers that 'one who does not speak in tongues is guilty of withholding a full surrender of the self to the will and purpose of God.' "

The Holy Spirit comes to us always in the Word and the Sacraments.
The Holy Spirit is an agent of conversion.
It is wrong to think we only get a "taste" of the Holy Spirit at Baptism and Conversion, and then a "big dose" when we speak in tongues.
It is true that we *do* grow in grace, we mature as Christians, and as we do, more and more of the Holy Spirit is evidenced in our lives. But it is grave error and mistake to say we get a "little" of the Holy Spirit at conversion, and a "lot" later. He, the Holy Spirit, who is God, cannot be so segmented.

Some of the world's greatest saints spoke in tongues. Paul was certainly one, Tertullian was another, Oral Roberts is a present-day charismatic. On the other hand, great men of God like Wesley, Luther, Augustine, Moody, Asbury, or Calvin, so far as we know, never spoke in tongues. This is simply to say — to speak, or not to speak in tongues — is not a criterion for judging the Spirit's presence and power in our lives.

We *do* know that one of the works of the Holy Spirit is to manifest Christ, so when a Christian is busy making Jesus known, and seen — then that person has the Holy Spirit.

The young children of a certain church were placing the figures of the nativity scene at Christmas time outside their church. One of the girls had arranged, and then re-arranged the manger several times. When someone asked her why she was spending so much time on it she replied: "We want to be sure that Jesus shows!" *That is* one of the best possible ways to know if the Holy Spirit indwells you: Are you showing Jesus in your life?

This, then, also answers the question that arises often:

DOES IT MAKE YOU A "BETTER CHRISTIAN" TO SPEAK IN TONGUES?

No, it does not! Paul, in 1 Corinthians mentions nine gifts of the Spirit. He says we should "earnestly desire the 'best' gifts." But as he names them, speaking in tongues and interpretation of tongues, are last on the list. What is the best gift? Obviously, the gift that is needed at a particular time, in that moment is the "best" gift. The best gift in one situation may not be the best in another time. Is it not reasonable to assume that there are times when the gift of faith is the invaluable gift, another instance may need the gift of wisdom, another time the gift of prophecy is the gift to be desired. Besides, it is just naturally offensive and opposed to all our Christian teaching for us to say that any gift of God would make us "better" than another. There is an ugly pride and arrogance that would claim spiritual superiority over another just because he speaks in tongues while another does not. If any gift of God should be ours for a given time, it should begin by making us very humble and very thankful, but never to think we are better.

Christ quickly withdraws himself from the person who claims a piety above and beyond someone else.

In a church where the chancel window, depicting Christ, had been removed for repair, a pastor asked a little child who was leaving the service one morning how she liked the worship service. She said: "O.K., but I sure did miss having Jesus with us!"

That's what we miss when we see a "holier-than-thou" Christian. Jesus with him!! The other question involved with the valid gift of speaking in tongues is

SHOULD YOU "SEEK" THE GIFT OF TONGUES?

To speak in tongues, just for the sake of "doing" it, is a low motivation and the poorest of reasons. It makes a little thing out of a great experience.

The story is told of a man named Wahlstrom. He had purchased an old bombsight. He took it apart to see what it was like, and when he put it together again he added some extra parts. He became utterly fascinated with this new pasttime. Neighbors began to bring in miscellaneous parts of machinery for his use. He went on expanding the mechanism. For ten years he kept putting together wheels, cogs, belts, and bolts; as a result he ended up with a machine people called "Wahlstrom's Wonder." When he threw a switch over 3,000 parts began to move, bells rang, lights flashed, belts from big wheels ran small wheels. There was just one problem — when you asked him what it does — here is his answer: "Oh, it doesn't do anything, it just runs!"

THAT is what speaking in tongues, for tongues sake alone, is — it is just running.

If God wants you to speak in tongues he will give you the gift.

And he will give it to you without requiring of you any strange manipulation of your tongue, repetition of certain words, or hysterics. These methods either give you no gift at all, or a false gift, or a gift of the Devil! We should always seek the gifts of the Spirit which will enrich our lives and our ministry to serve God and witness for him.

WHEN SHOULD YOU SPEAK IN TONGUES?

If you are given the gift of speaking in tongues, when should you do it?

Are you to exercise the gift anytime you please, whenever you feel like it?

If someone comes to you and says, "Speak, speak in tongues, I want to hear you!" —

Can you do it?

Of course you can't — at least not authentically. For, remember the gift is not yours; it is a gift which the *Spirit* gives, as Paul says, for use "as he wills or chooses."

You can "quench" the Spirit; you can, by yourself, turn it *OFF*, but not *ON* by yourself. The gift of tongues is no more yours to keep than are the other gifts of the Spirit which God may allow you to use from time to time: faith, healing, miracles, wisdom, etc.

There does seem to be a limited, good use of tongues in public worship. The gift of tongues, Paul teaches in 1 Corinthians 14, is to be used in public worship only when an interpreter is present. Then, he says, it is to be used only two, or at the most, three times. "Tongues are for an example to the unbeliever," Paul says, "but if you get together and all you do is talk in tongues, they will think you are mad." We must conclude, therefore, that there *is* a place in public worship for speaking in tongues, but it must be used in wisdom, in propriety, and properly.

There is the use of tongues in private worship — in prayer. Paul speaks in Romans 8:26, 27 of the Spirit helping us to pray. We don't always know how to pray as we ought, but the Spirit helps us with groanings which cannot be uttered. Now, this is perhaps the most helpful and also the most neglected area of speaking in tongues! God allows us to wrestle in prayer on behalf of situations, and of others and their needs. Have you not had times when your concern, your burden, your desire for another's good was so great you simply did not know how to pray or what to say? Have you not, at that time, gone to God in earnest prayer — and literally wept, groaned, wrestled, agonized, often inarticulately, in prayer for the need? This is not new; the Psalmist said: "He that goeth forth weeping, bearing precious seed, shall doubtless come again with rejoicing, bringing his sheaves with him." The prophet said: "When "Zion travails, she brings forth" — indicating that all good, all new birth, comes of travail, groaning, agonizing of spirit, weeping, labor. How long has it been since you were so concerned over some member of your family, some soul in the community who was unconverted, that you groaned and wept and found words fail — and in that inarticulate utterance made your way to God in prayer on that person's behalf? Now that's the way souls are won, the way the lost are found, the way lives are changed, the way situations are remedied. That's the way the Spirit wants to pray through you in an unknown tongue. Now there is a gift that any of us can well use. This is a far cry from the easy, light, casual, superficial praying that we usually do — praying that touches neither our own hearts, nor the heart of God. This is praying that will not let go, that will not be denied, that avails! So — the future may find you giving a "message in tongues" in public worship, or maybe you never will, but you can speak to God in a tongue that changes lives and situations.

— AND EVERYBODY SHOULD SEEK THAT GIFT!

For Losers And Cowards

Now the angel of the Lord came and sat under the oak at Ophrah, which belonged to Joash the Abiezrite, as his son Gideon was beating out wheat in the wine press, to hide it from the Midianites. And the angel of the Lord appeared to him and said to him, "The Lord is with you, you mighty man of valor." And Gideon said to him, "Pray, sir, if the Lord is with us, why then has all this befallen us? And where are all his wonderful deeds which our fathers recounted to us, saying, 'Did not the Lord bring us up from Egypt?' But now the Lord has cast us off, and given us into the hand of Midian." And the Lord turned to him and said, "Go in this might of yours and deliver Israel from the hand of Midian; do not I send you?" And he said to him, "Pray, Lord, how can I deliver Israel? Behold, my clan is the weakest in Manasseh, and I am the least in my family." And the Lord said to him, "But I will be with you, and you shall smite the Midianites as one man."

—*Judges 6:11-16*

You know what a "loser" is, don't you?

A loser is a woodpecker in a petrified forest.

A loser is a guy who sticks his hand out to make a left turn and smacks a traffic cop in the face.

A loser is a guy who plays hide-and-seek and nobody goes to look for him.

That's what Gideon was — a real "loser," before he teamed up with God. This story is a lesson for all losers, all little people, all those who feel they are too timid to ever be brave, all insignificant people, all fearful people, all defeated people — for all those who discount themselves and either have given up completely — or are just ready to throw in the towel.

Gideon is so much like us that his story, out of the Old Testament, sounds like some poor character in a best-selling paperback in today's book store. The nation of Israel has done wickedly, they've turned from worshipping the Jehovah God to idol worship, and as a result, God has allowed them, for seven years, to be harrassed by their enemies. These enemies include the Midianites, the Amalekites, and the people of the east.

Every time Israel plants a crop, these enemies come in and plunder and destroy it. The enemy has camels. And they run so fast, are so powerful, that the poor Israelites don't stand a chance. So the people are reduced to abject poverty, they hide in caves, they cower when the Midianite hordes descend upon them; and finally cry to God for help. This, then, is the existing situation when Gideon enters the account. How like us he seems!

GIDEON DIDN'T HAVE MUCH CONFIDENCE IN HIMSELF

When we first see Gideon, he is hiding in a cave, hoping the Midianites won't find him. Most of the crops have been plundered and destroyed, but what he has somehow managed to save must now be winnowed. So Gideon is in a cave, threshing wheat in a wine press, trying to get enough grain for flour for food. He's doing his job in the worst possible way. To winnow wheat you need to be out in the open air where the wind can blow the chaff away as the grain is tossed upward, leaving the good grain. But he's scared to be seen out in the open — so he's doing the best job he can, in hiding.

Then — one moment, probably when he stops long enough to wipe the dust out of his eyes and the sweat from his brow — he glances over the way, into the distance, and sees — of all things, an angel sitting under the oak tree!

And the angel speaks and says: "The Lord is with you, thou mighty man of valor!" (Now here's an angel with a crazy, mixed-up sense of humor. It doesn't look like God is even close to helping Gideon with his presence, and to call him a man of valor is impossibly funny. Gideon knows he isn't brave, in fact, he's frightened half out of his wits.)

And God says further, through the angel, "Go, save your people!" and Gideon's response is what you might expect under the circumstances: "Who, me? How? Why? My family is the poorest of the tribe and I'm the weakest and least in the family."

"But," the Lord said, "I will be with you!" (That's probably the best news Gideon has heard in something like seven years).

And Gideon said: "Oh, yeah, prove it." "But first, stay here and I'll go get you something to eat." (At least he didn't forget his manners altogether.) And he went home and fixed a meal for his visitor: roast young goat (Yuk!), broth, and bread. He gave it to the angel, still sitting under the oak tree — who told him to put it on a rock — and it was suddenly and miraculously consumed by fire — and then the angel disappeared!

Then it dawned upon Gideon, that he had really been talking to God (and he's not sure but that he may die from the experience) — and God says again: "Gideon, you won't die, but here is what I want you to do. Start restoring Jehovah worship to the land, tear down the altar of Baal, cut down the wooden idol of the goddess Asherah, replace Baal's altar with an altar to Me, put an ox on it as a sacrifice, and use the wooden idol you

destroy to make the wood on the fire for God's altar."
And Gideon did it.

But doesn't Gideon's lack of confidence in himself remind
you of us? Some of you may be very certain and sure of
yourself; you have no fears, no insecurities, no feelings of
inferiority, but if so, you are in the minority. Most of us,
if we know ourselves at all, admit that we don't have too
much self-confidence.

We are not even sure we would be missed by too many
people if we moved, or died.

There was a man who patronized a certain service
station. A boy named George occasionally checked his
oil, washed his windshield and filled his gas tank. One
day the motorist stopped for gas and didn't see George.
The next time he stopped at the station, George was not
there — nor the third time — so he asked the manager:
"Where's George?" The manager replied: "George
doesn't work here anymore." The customer said, "Who's
going to fill his vacancy?" The manager replied: "George
didn't *leave* any vacancy!"

Isn't that a pretty good picture of us? Who would miss us
if we didn't show up for work, for church, or a party to
which we were invited? Who are we, after all? There is
always someone richer, or younger, or smarter, or
stronger, or prettier than we are.

A man went to his psychologist because he suffered from
an inferiority complex. "Help me," he said to the doctor.
After a long series of tests and treatments the
psychologist reported to his patient, "I have good news
for you. You do not have a complex. You really are
inferior!" Yes, Gideon's feelings are as modern as today's
humanity. He said, "I'm the weakest in my family and my
family is the poorest in the tribe."

Like us, Gideon had little confidence in himself, but also

GIDEON DIDN'T HAVE MUCH FAITH IN GOD

One day, after the angel's visit with Gideon, the Midianites, Amalekites, and the other enemy nations gathered together — preparing for an all-out attack on Israel again —

And God told Gideon he was to deliver his people.

Gideon told God: "If you really mean to use me, prove it — I've got to have another sign. Tonight, I'll put some wool on the threshing floor; in the morning let the fleece be wet and the floor be dry."

Sure enough! The next morning God had confirmed it by doing just as Gideon had asked.

But — Gideon really wanted to be absolutely sure. (Just how sure do you have to be?) God has already visited him with an angel that talks to him and consumes food miraculously with fire on the rock, has helped him to destroy the altars of Baal and Asherah, has made the fleece wet and the floor dry all around it — but still Gideon wants more proof.

So Gideon says: "Now, God, don't get mad, but let's do it just one more time — only this time the other way around — in the morning let the fleece be dry and the floor wet all around it."

And God did that for him too.

Gideon's lack of faith in God has become a popular way of proving something yet today. When we want to test something to the limit we say we "put out a fleece."

Doesn't Gideon's lack of faith in God look familiar? God puts thousands of promises for us in the Bible; and we are not sure he means to keep them.

God promises if we ask we shall receive when we pray;

but we doubt him most of the time.

God has never, not even one time, failed us, but we keep expecting it to happen.

Oral Roberts says, "Something good is going to happen to you" — and we respond fearfully by saying, "Well, I hope so."

Or Oral Roberts says, "Expect a miracle" — and we, like Gideon, say, "Who, me? Prove it!"

And this loser named Gideon had still another problem:

GIDEON DIDN'T HAVE MUCH HUMAN HELP

Now, at least more convinced than he was, Gideon gets him an army together to fight the Midianites. God has showed him the miracles, the enemy is preparing an attack, and Gideon gathers some 32,000 soldiers to fight the battle. But God said, "That's too many men, Gideon. You'll think you won the battle all by yourself, so send the scared ones home." And 22,000 of them left, leaving only 10,000 to fight. God said, "That's still too many; "I'll sort them out for you. So down by the river, God thinned the ranks till Gideon wound up with only a pitifully small army of 300 men to do battle with the vast armies of the Midianites. Not much human help, is there? If Gideon is depending on man-power alone, he is doomed to failure. Three hundred men is almost no army at all!

There will be a lot of times in your life when, like Gideon, you will feel you have little human aid. You will be a minority, your friends won't always understand you, you may live life with thousands of acquaintances and friends, but when the going is hard, when the battle is rough, you will probably be able to count on the fingers of one hand those who will really stand by you.

An elderly lady in Florida said, "When my sister died, the last person on earth who cared about me was gone. I don't even have anybody to put in the blank space on my identification card in my wallet whom to notify in case of emergency."

But, however small your human helpers and resources are, remember that God always gives you somebody.

And beyond that he gives his Word: "*I* will never leave you nor forsake you, *I* will be with you always."

GIDEON DIDN'T HAVE MUCH EQUIPMENT

When Gideon and his band of 300 men started to fight the hordes of the Midianites, they realized they didn't have any real weapons of warfare. All they had were trumpets, clay jars, torches, and shouts!

But, the sounding of the trumpets, the breaking of the pitchers, the blazing of the torches, the shouting of the men — frightened the enemy half out of their wits, and they ran, terrified — stumbling over one another, and killing each other as they fled.

That day — with such puny resources of their own — Gideon and his men won the battle for the nation and for God!

Haven't you noticed how paltry your resources often are? Moses had only a rod in his hand. the little boy had only five loaves and two fishes; but it was enough — a little is a lot in God's large hands!

You feel you can't teach too well, or sing too well, you're not well-educated, you can't speak in public, you haven't much money, or strength. But what, after all, does it matter, how limited your resources are? In God's hands they mean the final defeat of the enemy.

Now — don't you see how modern Gideon's story is? Not much confidence in himself, not much faith in God, not much human help, not many resources; but the end result is what is important. And when the narrative ends you see Gideon has led the victory over the enemy,
    honor has come to him,
        peace has come to the whole land for the 40 years he
        lives
            and it was not by chance,
                nor by luck,
                    nor by coincidence
There were some vital essentials that were needed to make it work that way. You don't turn from being a loser into a winner without any effort.

You don't turn from being a coward into a brave person without meeting some requirements.

What Gideon needed — had to have, in fact — we must have also.

GIDEON NEEDED ASSURANCE

Gideon needed assurance, and re-assurance. God had to keep talking "faith" into him, helping him, encouraging him, proving himself to him — and we have to have the same thing. Most of us can believe God will help Billy Graham, Oral Roberts, the preacher, or some saintly person we know — but me?

A young woman came to her pastor with the question: "How can I believe that God is interested in what happens to me?" He answered, "Look at your fingers. There are billions of finger tips in the world, but no others are like yours. Even such a small detail has had the special attention of God."

Just as we need the constant assurance of parents, lover, husband, wife that we are "loved" — so we need the reassurance of God that we are not lost in the crowd of creation.

GIDEON NEEDED TO OBEY

If Gideon had not obeyed God he would probably have died in a cave — trying to winnow wheat in a wine press, fearful every moment of his life that the enemy was going to destroy him. We absolutely must (if we are to be anything but losers) learn to obey God!

God cannot use us, nor help us, nor change us until he first has explicit obedience from us. Without obedience we only bungle up and blunder around the plan of God for us. This is why we consider it imperative that our children obey us. It is not because we "dictate" to them, but it is for their security, their safety, their success in life. No matter how handsome a child is, nor how bright, nor how clever, nor how cute — that child is a mess until it knows how to mind. We, the children of God, are no different.

Archibald Rutledge told the story of meeting a Negro turpentine worker whose faithful dog had just died a few moments earlier in a great forest fire. The dog died because he would not desert his master's dinner pail which he had been told to watch. With tears raining down his face, the old black man said, "I always had to be so careful what I told him to do, 'cause I knowed he'd do it."

Wouldn't it do something fine to the great heart of God if he could find us just that faithfully obedient to what he tells us to do? Did you know that God expects obedience and honors obedience above sacrifice — and we weaken ourselves when we refuse to mind God?

GIDEON NEEDED THE RIGHT GOD

The Israelites had made all kinds of gods for themselves. God said, "Get rid of them!" — "tear down the altar to Baal — burn up the wooden idol of Asherah." God is a jealous God and he won't run in competition with other idols and gods. We are ingenious in the multiplication of our gods today. We make gods of anything and everything: our children, our home, our car, our job, money, prestige, power — idols of secularism, materialism — we've substituted so many things for God that we don't even know who God is anymore.

My preacher husband, John, and I were in a certain church in north Georgia, recently. John was preaching in the morning worship service. They have a procession, including the choir and pastors and all enter the chancel area by way of the center aisle. So, this morning, here they came: the robed choir, the pastor in his black Wesleyan robe, the associate minister in his black robe, and finally my John, following them. He wore a white alb, cincture, stole, large pectoral cross — which was all totally new to the pastor's six-year old daughter who sat in the second seat from the front. She has never seen a white-robed minister, the alb was new to her, the preacher a stranger, and she stood right up in front of everybody, and in a more-than-loud whisper said: "Who's that? What's that?" Then, apparently figuring it out for own satisfaction, she sat down and answered her own question, saying, "Oh, I know who that is, that's God!"

Some people are just that confused as to who God is for them. The awesome fact is that whatever is first in your life is also your God. Whatever or whoever receives priority from us is God to us! Until God is God, until you have the right God, you can never be anything but a loser!

GIDEON NEEDED REPENTANCE

The absolutely indispensible ingredient for curing cowardice, littleness, and defeat is repentance. Before God could ever do anything to help Gideon and the nation there had to be deep sorrow for their sins, a return to God, a genuine repentance. They cried to the Lord, they repented, and he heard them.

How long has it been since your sins bothered you so much that you wept before God about them?

We handle sin so lightly, so casually, so easily rationalizing and excusing ourselves by saying: "Oh, well, I'm only human" or "Everybody does it, I'm no worse than anyone else," or, flippantly: "The devil make me do it!"

When we do wrong we sin against a holy God and we need to repent.

One of the terrible things we need to understand is people *are* sinners — but even worse than that is that we are sinners and refuse to admit it.

The most basic fact about humanity is that we are sinful, born in sin. Our most desperate need is for a Savior. Nothing else will do. We've tried all kinds of substitutes and delaying tactics to circumvent repentance for sin. But people and plans fail us.

Let a person go to a psychiatrist to cure his sins — and all you get is an adjusted sinner.

Let a person go to a physician to cure the disease of sin — and you get a *healthy* sinner.

Let a person achieve wealth — and you have an affluent sinner.

Let a person join a church, sign a card, turn over a new leaf, and you have a religious sinner.

But let a person come in sincere repentance and faith to the foot of the cross of Jesus Christ, confessing his sins — and you have a forgiven sinner. You have a new creature, reconciled, redeemed, and different. There is simply no way for our multitudinous problems to be remedied until we deal with the basic issue — we have sinned, and need to repent.

YOU MATTER TO GOD

Isn't Gideon's story marvelously comforting and encouraging?

You don't need to be a loser any longer.

You may not matter to everyone, but you matter to God!

The prescription to effect your cure was written in the red blood of Calvary's Cross — and all those receiving that treatment are made completely whole.

Hooray for Humility!

Let this mind be in you, which was also in Christ Jesus ... He humbled himself, and became obedient unto death, even the death of the cross.
Philippians 2:5, 8

My husband John tells of attending a football game a few seasons back in Knoxville, Tennessee, where the battle was between Army and the University of Tennessee. Before the game started, there were some preliminary features. Each side showed off his mascot. UT proudly displayed a beautiful high-stepping horse. A pretty young girl, dressed in riding garb, rode it around the stadium. The horse's tail was high, his head held high, he lifted his legs proudly as he trotted around the area to the applause of some 60,000 fans in attendance. It was a picture of majesty, glory, and pride.

When the UT mascot left the field, the crowd then saw Army's mascot — a mule! He was dressed in a drab army blanket. He plodded unwillingly about, and when they tried to move him off the playing field, he refused to budge. Finally they got him out of sight with one cadet pulling on his bridle and the other pushing from behind. The mule was a sorry contrast to the wonderful stallion — a vivid picture of the contrast between pride and humility.

The early church named seven deadly sins, but said they all originate in pride. Pride is the source of all evil, the opposite of true humility.

Note the humility in the story of the time a Mr. William Allen White, one-time dean of all newspapermen in America, was awarded an honorary degree by Columbia

University. At the commencement, a quiet, unassuming man stood next to him in the regal and colorful academic procession. Mr. White turned to the man beside him and in a humble and friendly manner, completely without pride, said: "We ought to get to know each aother. I'm a small town editor from Emporia, Kansas, My name is White." The quiet man replied: "I'm a small town doctor from Rochester, Minnesota. My name is Mayo." Beautiful, isn't it?

The humility of those two men stands in marked contrast to the principal who said to his secretary: "The trouble with some people is that they don't admit their faults. I'd admit mine — if I had any!"

Following a revival service, a few weeks past, a man shook my hand and told me that a few years ago he had written a series of three papers on humility. Then he added: "I'd like for you to read them, they are really very good!"

Just as pride is our downfall, humility is the greatest grace! It is one of the fairest and rarest flowers that blooms in the garden of God. Humility is often misunderstood. It is not an abject and grovelling spirit. Humility is not self-deprecation. Humility is not self-attained, it is God-given. Humility is best seen in Jesus Christ. Look at how he practiced and taught it.

JESUS' HUMILITY IS MANIFESTED

"He humbled himself and became obedient unto death." This is an important doctrinal statement concerning Jesus. William Barclay says "it is the greatest and most moving passage that Paul ever wrote about Jesus."

This really is the climax of humiliation — the cross! But it started long before the cross.

Christ was always doing the humble thing.

He started out by God becoming man — by leaving heaven to come down to earth. He was born in a barn instead of a palace. He lived on earth without a home of his own. Even in the parade in which he was the principal character (We Christians call it Palm Sunday), he was unbelievably humble. It was a rather second-rate parade, when you stop to think about it. No prancing Arabian horse to ride — just an unbroken colt. No greenhouse flowers — just dandelion-type wildflowers thrown in his path. No fancy robes and royal regalia — just the usual, dusty seamless robe, woven for him, perhaps by his mother. No "big-name" people in the parade, no mayor of the town, no visiting "media personality" — just children and peasants and disciples. The people cheered — but he cried at his own parade: embarrassed those who followed him, probably, when his shoulders began to shake with sobs, and tears ran down his face — and they remembered a prayer: "O Jerusalem, Jerusalem — how oft would I have gathered you — but you would not, you would not!" And not many days later he is stooping down to wash his disciples feet —

and now —
    now Paul comes to the grand climax of a life of humiliation: DEATH ON A CROSS!

This would be intensely moving to the Philippians. They were Romans, citizens of a Roman colony with special Roman rights. Neither Paul, nor the Philippians, could ever be sentenced to death by crucifixion. It was too humiliating a death for a Roman. Oh, can you believe it? Too humiliating for a *Roman* citizen, but *Heaven's* chief Citizen chooses to thus die!

But then, Christ was always doing the unexpected thing.
    His people looked for a champion on a charger, he came a child in the straw.

They expected outer revolution from him, he came to give inner redemption.
They wanted freedom through insurrection, he offered liberty by way of a cross.

Such humility! The God who became man emptied himself of Divine privileges and made the awesom sacrifice of death on a cross-tree!

JESUS' HUMILITY IS TO BE IMITATED

"Let this mind be in you which also was in Christ Jesus." Yes, that really is what it says: "think just as Jesus thought."
He humbled himself,
    now you do it too.

Many proponents of the women's lib movement have revolted against the idea of humility, of submission, servanthood, saying they cannot "be their own persons" and "do their own thing" as servants. And yet, Christ, the Divine Son of God humbled himself and became a servant, obedient unto death, the terrible death of the cross. Can we ever think we are above our Lord?

Martin Luther said, concerning humility: "God created the world out of nothing. As long as you are not yet nothing, God cannot make something out of you."

Humility is hard to attain — the moment we think it is ours — it is gone. Did you hear about the student who was awarded a gold pin for being the most humble man in his college class — but it was taken away from him the next day because he wore it?

We don't become humble on our own — the grace is God-given. It results from a sense of our own sinfulness. It is seeing God as great, holy, clean, pure, good; and then seeing ourselves in contrast. It is also recognition that all that is good about you really comes from God. Every virtue we catch in ourselves should make us grateful, not proud.

Egotism and pride go hand in hand. Pride is the villain in almost all the parables Jesus told. Pride is the sin of so-called "good" people, and strikes where we smugly assume we are strongest. Pride was the devil's real trouble. Lucifer didn't "run-around," didn't "over-indulge." His sin was in wanting God's seat.

Remember the Pharisee in the story Jesus told?
   In two short verses the Pharisee used the pronoun "I" five times.
He had a *proud* eye on himself,
   a *judgmental* eye on the Publican,
      and *no* eye on God at all! Listen to him: "God *I* thank thee that *I* am not as other men are . . . *I* fast twice in the week, *I* give tithes of all that *I* possess." The *I* in many of us goes on and on, ad infinitum, ad nauseum. Our only hope is to be like the poor publican, praying over in a corner. He knows how badly he is infected, how much he needs help, how "at-the-end-of-his-rope" he is. And he prays a prayer we would do well to imitate every day: "God, be merciful to me a sinner!" The proud Pharisee reminds us of the proud male Jew of earlier days who used to pray each morning: "God, I thank thee that thou hast not made me a Gentile, a slave, or a woman."

Contrast that proud prayer with the modesty and humility of the great Albert Einstein, who having hit on his Theory of Relativity equation; $E=mc2$ — came downstairs in his sweatshirt and bedroom slippers one morning and said: "Mamma, I have a little new idea."

Paul says, in the text, "Think just as Jesus thought" — and he humbled himself.

There is a beautiful story concerning the singing of the "Hallelujah Chorus" in Albert Hall, London. Early in her reign, the young Victoria, Queen of England, sat in her royal box, listening to Handel's inspired music, the *Messiah*. One of her attendants came to her, advising her that when the great chorus was sung, the audience would rise, but since she was a queen it would be perfectly proper etiquette for her majesty to remain seated. However, as the choir reached that glorious climax with the words; "King of Kings, and Lord of Lords," the young queen suddenly stood with her head bowed, indicating to all present that she knew the real sovereign of England, the true ruler of the world!

JESUS' HUMILITY IS THE CURE FOR DISUNITY

"Christ became obedient unto death" — "as ye have always obeyed, work out your own salvation with fear and trembling." If the humility of Christ could be imitated in all our lives, we would never again have disunity, division, and fightings within the body of Christ!

In fact, Paul wrote this marvelous passage in Philippians because he wanted to heal the problems of disunity within the church at Philippi.

We are not strangers to division within our church today. *Denominations* suffer from disunity. There is not a major Christian denomination that has not felt the ravages of disunity in its ranks in the last decade. But *denominations* are not the only troubled ones — *the local church* has suffered factions, fractious members, and divisions within it. For that matter, we could be more personal, and ask: "What *family* do you know that has total harmony in it?" And sometimes we are so divided we cannot get along with our own *self!* One man said: "I am a walking civil war." The fact is, we are capable of splitting, arguing, and disagreeing over almost anything — over baptism, communion, speaking in tongues, the gender of the clergy, the raising of the budget, or what color of new carpet to buy.

Steven McNeil used to tell about two of the blind men whom Jesus healed. They met one day and started talking — comparing notes about how it happened that they were healed of blindness. Said one: "Of course, Jesus put mud on your eyes and had you go wash in the pool of Siloam." "Of course not!" said the second man, "He simply said, 'Receive your sight!' " "You mean," the first continued, "he didn't put mud on your eyes?" "Certainly not!" "Then," the first retorted, "you are still blind!" (And so another fuss began.)

Paul calls for humility and union on the basis of Christ's humility. Paul warns us of the causes of disunity: selfish ambition, desire for personal prestige, concentration on self."

He says: "Do your good works, not for personal advancement, but simply because you are "*in Christ*." We would do well to examine our motives in Christian service. Ask yourself: "Would I do the good things in church I am doing if no one else knew about it?" Do you have to "tell" how you cleaned up the kitchen, took the nursery two Sundays in a row, gave above your pledge, what class you taught, what you "said" that helped somebody?

In a church I served as pastor there was a dear saint who gave a pulpit Bible anonymously; the next year gave a new piano to the church; the next year an organ to enhance the worship services; and never let me tell who did it! Marvelous humility, isn't it? You can do a lot of good if you don't care who gets the credit. Keep in mind that the aim of the Christian is not self-display, but self-obliteration. Christ humbled himself to death on a cross,

can we humble ourselves to death that hides behind that same cross?

We might be able to better illuminate the way to God if we could ever stop our quarreling, our dis-union, and fractiousness.

A blind man, tapping a white cane along a busy city sidewalk, stopped near a group of people and asked directions to the museum. "Museum?" asked one man — "Why you take the next corner to your left." "No," objected another man, "you take the second corner on your right." "You are both wrong," stated a young woman, "if you keep straight ahead for about three blocks you will run directly into the museum." The other person in the group murmured simply, "I haven't the faintest idea where it is." At that moment a policeman appeared and said: "Sorry, but you people will have to move along. You're all blocking the entrance to the museum!"

How often have we blocked the way to heaven by our disunity; because of it some seeking soul has lost his way.

HOORAY FOR HUMILITY

Humility would cure so many ills, heal so many divisions, bless so many lives, enrich us to immeasurably.

Today as on Palm Sunday, our Hosannas are for the King of Humility.

Our greatness must always lie in what *Christ* has done, not in what *we* are. The truth is it is all that God will accept from us!

A story is told of the funeral of Charlemagne, one of the greatest early rulers of the earth. The mighty funeral procession came to the cathedral, only to find the gate barred by the bishop, representative for God.

"Who comes?" shouted the bishop.

The heralds answered, "Charlemagne, Lord and King of the Holy Roman Empire!"

The bishop replied, for God, "Him I know not! — Who comes?"

The heralds, a bit shaken, replied, "Charles the Great, a good and honest man of earth!"

Again the bishop answered, "Him I know now! — Who comes?"

Now, completely crushed, the heralds give answer, "Charles a lowly sinner, who begs the gift of Christ."

Then God's representative said, "Him I know! Enter! Receive Christ's gift of enternal life!"

We really are nothing . . .

Christ really is everything . . .

HOORAY FOR HUMILITY!

When Love Runs Out of Breath

And one of them, a lawyer, asked him a question, to test him. "Teacher, which is the great commandment in the law?" And he said to him, "You shall love the Lord your God with all your heart, and with all your soul, and with all your mind. This is the great and first commandment. And a second is like it, You shall love your neighbor as yourself."

Matthew 22:35-39

The usher, showing me the way to the pastor's study, wore a big, bright, round button on his lapel which read: "I love you — Is that O.K.?" I didn't know him, he only knew that I was the visiting preacher in the pulpit that day, so, after re-reading his button, I said; "Yes, I think it's O.K." His reaction was immediate: he ducked his head, blushed to his ears, and in a choked voice said: "Ah, oh, uh, well, that's good." Why would anybody wear a button that said that to everybody?

"Easy love" — we say we love small, long-haired dogs, we love sporty cars, we love split-level houses, we love sharp clothes, we love pop songs, we love *some* people, we love the colors of blue and yellow, we love faded jeans, and we love dimpled babies — or anything else you can think of! Love is the most overworked, misunderstood, least-practiced word of our time! The whole subject of love is too big for us, and the practice of it is almost completely beyond us.

Think of what love is not:
  Hugs and kisses and squeezes,
    Little gifts to the United Fund, Red Cross, and Easter Seal Drive,
      Songs about love,
        Banners and buttons,

Posters and cute little cartoon figures with impish, childish faces,
Easy sentimentality,
Doing what is convenient (because it is "expected of us," or someone will remark how "good" we are),
Something nice you do till you get tired of it, or think it's "someone else's turn" for awhile,
A pat on the back and "have a nice day",
And of course love is never, never jealous, selfish, irritable, resentful, rude, or proud!

But think of what *love is:*
Tough,
Hard,
Eternal (it goes on and on and on and on against impossible odds),
Taking people *where* they are, *as* they are,
Being kicked, and not kicking back,
Patient, longsuffering, and kind,
Real (not fake, or imitation, or put-on, or make-believe, or pretend),
Unprejudiced (you will help the person who needs it even if he is: under 30 — or over 30, Republican or Democrat, Methodist or Protestant or Catholic or no church at all!,
Grateful or ungrateful,
a somebody or a nobody,
Wow! — all of that? that's really unprejudiced!)
Forgiving,
Hopeful,
and love is impossible to do by yourself

But you already knew all this about love. You've given mental assent to it many times over. You believe it. But the hard, ugly truth is that even though we are Christians, we find that in theory all of this is fine, but in reality and in practice it just doesn't work out that way for us.

Most of us have made commitments to love before. We've gone to church and got all inspired — we are going to be different. We read the Bible a little more, we pray a couple more minutes each day, and go on a binge of "being a better Christian." And we make a high resolve for ourselves: We are going to love — really love — love all the time — and love everybody!

    And we do pretty well,
      until,
        one day we wake up with a bad headache,
          or a fresh cold,
            or we over-sleep and are late for work,
              or the children are difficult,
                or the milk for cereal is sour,
                  or the car won't start—
and whoever is closest to us really gets it! — Our reaction to some small trifle makes us talk and act like anything but loving — so we chuck the whole project, thinking, "It's no use anyway."

    And, in order to live with ourselves, we rationalize our failure by saying:
      "After all, I'm only human," or
        "Everyone feels this way sometimes," or
          "It's just not *natural* to be loving all the time," and once again we find our love is short of breath!

            We "tried" — we honestly "tried," but we can't be loving all the time. We are sick and tired of trying, we are sick of feeling guilty about it, we are ready to wash our hands of whole "loving" mess!

And you are right. This is as good a time as any to realize that you can never make yourself love.

Those people who easily and blithely say they "love everybody" are suspect in my book. Most of the time it's just words, words, words — and words about love are always easy! There is this one basic lesson that we keep forgetting: All your loving depends upon your present relationship to Christ.

Jesus said, in the words of this text in Matthew: "You shall love the Lord your God with all your heart, and with all your soul, and with all your mind. This is the first and great commandment. A second is like it. You shall love your neighbor as yourself."

Note the order that is given here — first we take care of the God-relationship, and then the human-relationship. And here our dilemma begins, for modern man has chosen to reverse this order. But it is impossible to love people (some people are so unloveable you can't even *like* them), unless you first love God.

Today's system is not Christian, but humanism. We've said: "Let man be center, let man be the focal point, let man be first, let man be pre-eminent." But this "human awareness" has cost us — we've lost our "God awareness," and as a result we soon don't care too much for God *or* man.

Until we truly love God, we can't really love man. The God-to-man, vertical relationship, must be sound before we can even start on the horizontal relationship, man-to-man, person-to-person. What has happened is that we start out very well on the horizontal basis. With great intentions we start to "love people" — only to find that some of them are so unloveable we can't stand them, so ungrateful we can't believe it, so unworthy that we start looking for "worthy people" — and our love is suddenly out of breath — our good intentions evaporate in the light of the human capability for being ugly, unappreciative, uncooperative, and impossible. So, like all the other times we have tried, we give up on this "loving everybody business" and decide it's for the mystics.

But if our loving begins with the Christ relationship — all is changed! We can't love each other until we know how much we, ourselves, are loved. And one big reason we don't realize how much we are loved is that we don't really know how bad we are to begin with, nor how much we desperately need love.

Did you ever notice how that (privately) we think we are pretty good,
  how "lucky" God is to have us in his church and in his
  service,
    how, compared to others, we are so outstanding? —
    and there is the problem — we've been comparing
ourselves with others. The Scripture already warns against that: "And they, comparing themselves by themselves, are unwise."

You can always find somebody to compare yourself with who will make you look great — there is always someone fatter than you are,
  older than you are,
  slower than you are,
  more sinful than you are,
  dumber than you are.
Sure! compared to others you look fine —
  of course, compared to Christ we look terrible,
    so we run back to human comparisons — so much
    safer and so much more comfortable.
So — we defeat ourselves. For not until we see *our* need, *our* sin, *our* badness, *our* wrong — can we ever see the

real need for God's grace and love and mercy. Most of the time we ignore or minimize our own sin-problem. After all, it's not "so bad." reminds me of the story that has come out of North Ireland. A fellow came from North Ireland to New York, and he was asked for a television interview about the conditions in his country. The interviewer asked the Irishman, "What's this we hear about all the violence and killing and bombing and fighting in Northern Ireland?" "Well," the man responded, "You know, it's really not so bad. You can't trust the press. The newspapers exaggerate. True, we've had some people driving through red lights. Some people double parking, a few arguments in pubs, but nothing very bad." The interviewer said: "Well, I'm awfully glad and relieved to hear you say that. We Americans thought it was pretty bad over there. By the way, what is your job in Northern Ireland just now?" And the man answered; "Well, for the last two years I've been the tail gunner on a milk wagon!"

Not so different from us, is it? We just shut our eyes to our sins and badness. We can diagnose the problems of the world, the church, the community, the government, and our neighbors — but our own needs we can't even see.

If God would help us to see our own pollution, then seeing our need, our desperate need for a loving Savior would naturally follow.

LOOK AT THE POLLUTION PROBLEM ALL AROUND US,

WE ARE PHYSICALLY POLLUTED

We have polluted our water until our beaches are unfit to use for swimming, our rivers and streams are contaminated until fishes die in unbelievable and uncountable numbers.

Our air is so polluted that our lungs are dirty gray and/or black. Major cities give a "pollution reading" as regularly as the temperature.

We have littered the land so badly that we pick up trash every year to the tune of 56 billion cans, 32 billion bottles, 34 million tons of paper — it cost a million and a half dollars to clean up Georgia highways last year. Our natural, instinctive reaction to such statistics is to say: "That's terrible, I would never contribute to that problem in our land."

WE ARE MENTALLY POLLUTED

As terrible as the physical pollution is, the mental is far worse. We read dirty books, tell dirty jokes, look at dirty movies, and think dirty thoughts. Then our actions reveal how dirty our thinking really is. A major city newspaper recently carried the story of six boys who raped a seventeen year old girl after they got her drunk, then when she became ill they allowed her to choke to death on her own vomit. That's dirty! That's pollution, but only one single incident from a society of people whose minds are polluted and whose actions betray them.

A newscaster told of a fifteen year old boy who had been caught as a rapist, but he tried to run from the police, and, in trying to escape, was shot and killed. The boy's mother came and shook the policeman's hand and said: "Thank you for killing my son. He's been arrested thirty-seven times in fifteen years. He didn't deserve to live, I'm glad he's dead."

How polluted can mankind get?

Again, our reaction to such vulgarity and criminality is to say: "But my actions and thoughts are not like that. I would never do anything so terrible — and so the comparison of self with others continues and our un-recognized need is covered again.

OUR HEARTS ARE POLLUTED

Sin is blinding. Jeremiah said; "The heart is deceitful and desperately wicked." David knew he could not trust his sinful heart any longer, so he cried out for God to create in him a new heart.

Once in awhile we catch a glimmer of truth as to just how capable of wrong we are. Really now, aren't you surprised at the things you are capable of saying to another person in sudden anger, aren't you surprised at what you can think, aren't you surprised at your desire to hurt, to cut, and to wound? If God would just be good enough to us to let us see how bad our own sins are, how great is our own need, how far short we come of the perfect example set for us in Christ — then we would probably cry out, as did Martin Luther: "Oh, my sins, my sins, my sins!"

Once Luther saw his sins — then he, with clear eye, could see the Savior. In his second article Luther wrote: ". . . Christ has redeemed me, a lost and condemned creature, secured and delivered me from all sins, from death, and from the power of the devil, not with silver and gold, but with his holy and precious blood, and with his innocent sufferings and death; in order that I might be his, live under him in his kingdom, and serve him in everlasting righteousness, innocence, and blessedness; even as he is risen from the dead, and lives and reigns to all eternity. This is most certainly true."

Then, when our need, and Christ's sufficiency dawns upon us — suddenly we are amazed, astounded, humbled. He puts up with me, loves me, accepts me, forgives me, saves me, lets me live.

I just love the old song we were taught as children:
"I am so glad that our father in heaven,
Tells of his love in the Book he has given;
Wonderful things in the Bible I see,
But this is the dearest, that Jesus loves me.

I am so glad that Jesus loves me,
Jesus loves me, Jesus loves me,
I am so glad that Jesus loves me,
(and I can hardly wait to get to the last line for it says:)
Jesus loves even me!"

Did you get that, "even me?" I can understand God loving someone like St. Francis, or my saintly mother, or my Christ-like husband, John, or a sweet little innocent baby — but me? — even me?

I just can't get over God — over that kind of love.

Now when that kind of love dawns upon us ... in gratitude to Christ for his love to me, I can now love others. They have not necessarily changed. They may still be unloving, dirty, ungrateful, worthless, not nice — they are the same, only now I am different.

I can love because I am loved!
Do you see why all your loving depends upon your present relationship to Jesus Christ?
I see Christ — I see my sins — I see me accepted in Christ — now I see others in a new light.

The story is told of a traveler in Africa who was watching a nun dressing the wounds of a leper. The sores were revolting, ugly, gruesome, repulsive, and stinking. As the traveler watched her, standing some distance away, he said: "I wouldn't do that for ten thousand dollars!" Without even bothering to look up the nun replied, "Neither would I!"

But what she would not do for money, she did willingly for love, for gratitude to one who had loved her and given himself for her. The next time you find your love running out of breath — run to the cross-tree, and there on a hill called Calvary see Divine love dying in agony and blood for your sins — and know and remember however sinful you are — you are loved anyway.

Breathe in deeply of the love of our dying Savior — then run quickly back to our world and breathe his love all over it!

Defended By the Divine

But Jesus said, "Let her alone; why do you trouble her? She has done a beautiful thing to me."
Mark 14:6

Women have sometimes had the reputation for doing some pretty dumb things. My preacher-husband, John, and I drove to a preaching mission in Mississippi recently. Three different times, the same day, we found ourselves behind a woman (a different one each time) who signaled to make a turn, then turned the opposite direction from her signal. It reminded me of the person who said "When a woman sticks out her arm, and indicates a left turn, the only thing you can be absolutely sure of is that the window is down!"

And women are often accused of having no economic sense (nobody really deserves such generalities). Untold cartoons have been drawn and stories told of women's inability to balance a checkbook. Blondie and Dagwood Bumstead comics have not done the reputation much good either. It has been said that a man will pay one dollar for a two dollar item if he needs it, but if it is on sale for two dollars and worth only one dollar, a woman will buy it whether she can use it or not!

Women are accused, too, of being overly sentimental. They cry at strange times — even happy occasions like graduations and weddings. Big things they handle calmly, then an unexpected small gift will break them up.

And logic — "the logic of a woman" is a proverb all its own! Well, here a woman is not negated, berated, accused, minimized, criticized, or put-down (which only proves how perfectly fair Christ always was. For had the same action been evidenced in a man, as it was in this case in a woman, his reaction would have been exactly the same. It is certainly not the "point" of this lesson, but it goes a long way toward teaching Christ's understanding of equality of men and women). Here, a woman named Mary, we call her now Mary of Bethany, is defended, judged and aquitted by none other than Jesus Christ, the Divine Son of God. He defends her actions — and calls them good.

But back to the beginning — The poignancy of this story lies in the fact that it tells us of almost the last kindness that was done to Jesus before his death.

He was in the house of a man called Simon, the village of Bethany. In Palestine, the people usually did not sit to eat — they reclined on low couches — resting one arm to support themselves, the other hand to take their food. So it was that anyone coming up to someone at mealtime would just naturally stand well above them. Mary came to Jesus with an alabaster vial of precious ointment. It was the custom to pour a few drops of perfume on a guest when he arrived at a house or when he sat down to a meal. This vial was nard, a very precious ointment from a rare plant that grew in India. But it was not just a few drops that this woman poured on the head of Jesus — she broke the flask and anointed him with the whole contents.

Then the criticisms began — the disciples and the others who saw her lavish action really threw a fit about it. After all, that flask was worth 300 denarii. It would have cost an ordinary man almost a year's pay to buy that flask of ointment — and here this dumb, sentimental, illogical, foolish woman is wasting it! You could give the money to the poor, you could save it, you could trade with it — and they turned the wrath of their judgment full upon her.

And Jesus reacted immediately too.

He comes promptly to her defense and says: "You let her alone. — I approve of what she has done. She did the right thing, it is a beautiful act. Stop judging her by your standards . . . let her alone — I like what she has done."

Now any act that Jesus applauds and approves deserves our special consideration. It means that perhaps we can learn from the example set and find ourselves defended by the Divine, as well. Look at some of the ways that Mary of Bethany's action could be called beautiful.

IT WAS BEAUTIFUL IN ITS MOTIVE

Mary acted out of a heart of pure love and devotion to her Lord. We need to learn, better than we have, how very important motives are, they make such a difference.

We need to ask ourselves about the "good" things we do — do we do them to be seen of others, or to perform a real service of devotion to God? Are we faithful and good and conscientious and hard-working so that people will say: "How loyal he is," or "You work harder than anyone else," or "What would we ever do without you," or "Nobody else would do what you are doing, you are *so* good!" Mary was not seeking the limelight — she had no idea she was going to be remembered down through time — for no reason, no reason other than love, she poured the ointment upon Jesus.

Examine the next service you perform for God, for the church, for someone and see what the motive is — is it pure and untainted by self-seeking or is it tarnished with desire for self-glory? Isn't that a terrifying question to ask about our good deeds?

Only you can interpret your motives — other people may misunderstand them entirely, for good is often done with a fine motivation, and we have been accused of ulterior reasons, while at other times the good is accomplished for a poor purpose, and we have been given full credit for the deed. You only can know the true motivation, for often the same act is performed with opposite motives. For instance, suppose the kiss of Judas had been for a different motive other than betrayal? Suppose Judas had kissed Jesus on the cheek, intending to say by that action, "I will be faithful, I'll stand by you, I'm your friend whatever happens, I offer you my full allegiance!" The act would have been identical with the kiss of betrayal — but the first deed would have been beautiful, the actual act was ugly and loathsome — motive made the difference!

What motivation sparks you as a Christian — do you want to be seen, praised, noticed, and honored? Or can you serve equally well without notice, in or out of the limelight, doing the service "unto God" and not having it matter one whit whether others even know about it or not?

Remember, you can do a lot of good for Christ if you don't mind who gets the credit!

IT WAS BEAUTIFUL IN ITS RECKLESSNESS

True love always has a certain extravagnace about it. There is a recklessness in love which refuses to count the cost. This woman took the most precious thing she had and literally lavished it upon Jesus. Jewish women were very fond of perfume (what woman isn't?) — and Mary just poured the whole bottle on Jesus!

It didn't seem to occur to her to think: "I'll give him a few extra drops, or a fourth of it, or half of it, and save some of it" — she just, with a kind of wild abandon, tipped it up, and gave him all of it!

How sad that we are often afraid of doing "too much." How many times, in looking for someone to do something in the local church, I've heard it said: "I've done my share," "I've given enough," "Let somebody else do it, I deserve a break."

If we are measuring our gifts or service by what others in the same situation have done or given, then maybe we have done enough — but if we are measuring them in the light of what's been done for us, when can we ever say we have "done enough?" In the light of the staggering sacrifice of the Cross, in recollection of all Christ suffered on our behalf, who of us can ever say: "I've done my share?"

You don't have to be reckless for God. There is always a way to get out of doing or giving if you really want to. You can find a way to be stingy for God if you look for it. Remember the story of the three Scotsmen who went to church together and everything was going just fine until the offering was taken. They immediately went into a whispered conference and solved the difficulty of facing the offering plate that was fast coming toward them — one of them fainted and the other two carried him out!

Contrast that, and our counting every little thing we do and give for Christ, with the feelings of Queen Victoria. Dean Farrar relates that Queen Victoria, after hearing one of her chaplains preach at Windsor Castle on the life and soon return of Christ, said to the dean; "Oh, how I wish the Lord would come during my lifetime." "Why does your Majesty feel this earnest desire?" asked the great preacher. Her countenance lit up with deep emotion as she replied, "Because I should so love to lay my crown at his feet."

Remember that the two always go together — the heart that loves and cares, and the gift that costs.

Sometime ago, a brother minister was telling a group about a new unit that was being added to his church. It was an expensive project, and was not going well at all, funds were very slow in coming in. Late that afternoon of the same week one of the elderly widow women in his parish stopped by his study. "I have a gift," she said, and rather timidly extended to her surprised pastor her wedding ring. "Sell it, and give the money to the church building fund," she said. Gaining control of himself, he said to her, "My dear lady, it's true we are not having an easy time completing this building, but we cannot accept you wedding ring. We'll manage somehow without a sacrifice like this!" "Oh, you do not understand," was her reply. "My husband has gone on to heaven. We are expanding our church plant to prepare people for eternity. I would not feel right unless I could give that which is the dearest I own!"

No wonder Jesus called Mary's devotion beautiful; the recklessness of it must have gladdened him greatly!

IT WAS BEAUTIFUL IN ITS UNIQUENESS

What Mary offered to Jesus was certainly different! No one else did this for him. Apparently she was the only one who even thought of it.

Not everyone can do the same thing.
   When will we ever learn that we don't have to do what others do. Maybe we can't.
   Not everyone has the same amount to give.

   Some can preach, or sing, or pray, or teach, or give, or wash dishes, or make phone calls, or type, or keep the nursery, or sew, and so on ad infinitum.
   The important thing is that you do what you can do!

In a revival recently, I was in the church, when I noticed the black custodian down on his knees, under the pews, with a dust cloth, dusting even under the pews, in the hard-to-get-places, making it clean everywhere. I commented on how thorough he was and he replied: "Mam, I can't do much, I can't give much, I don't know much — but I done decided I can give God the cleanest, best-smellin' church in town!" How about that for being beautiful and unique?

Love cannot always do what it wants to do — but love will do something.

Love has a way of finding a way.
Love has an ingenuity all its own. It is born of that high desire to give out of purity of heart, devotion, and of a spirit free and unencumbered with selfishness.

A crippled woman was the mother of three lovely little daughters, aged nine, seven, and three years. As the mother's birthday approached, the older girls saved their small allowances in piggy banks, and planned to make a big occasion of their mother's birthday with their little gifts. The day arrived and they had made their purchases. Holding a tray in her hands, the nine year old entered the living room first. On the tray was a small box of powder and a bottle of perfume. Standing before her mother's wheel-chair she exclaimed, "Happy Birthday, Mother, I give you this present." Then the seven year old came into the room. On her tray were some very simple kitchen utensils. "Happy Birthday, Mother," she said, "I give you these things to cook with." When the three year old came in with an empty tray in her hand, it suddenly occurred to her older sisters that they had not shared their pennies with her. And of course she was too young to save her own. But she walked straight up to the wheel chair. Placing the tray directly in front of the one she loved most, she stepped on top of her tray and stood there with her eyes shining bright: "Happy Birthday, Mommy," she whispered, "I give you me."

Don't complain about what you cannot give — give what you have. Others may call it strange, different, even peculiar — so what? Jesus will look at your loving gift and call it beautiful.

IT WAS BEAUTIFUL IN ITS TIMELINESS

Some things must be done when you have the opportunity —
    the chance may never come again.
        Love knows this better than anyone.
Often we are moved by some generous impulse, some good intention, and do not act upon it immediately, and the opportunity never affords itself another time.

This offering of Mary was one that was not "too late."

A woman called me long distance, lately, to tell me of the death of her mother. After expressing sympathy and condolences, I noted, as is often the case, that something other than grief was troubling her — guilt. She said: "I wish I had been kinder to her, done more things for her, visited her more often. I could have, but I thought I was too busy, now it's too late." — "Too late" — how often we use these words. We have the finest and best of intentions — but procrastinate in carrying them out — and then it is "too late."
    Jesus said, of Mary; "She hath come aforetime to annoint my body for burial."

Recall that there were other women who wanted to anoint his body for burial — that's why they were there on the dawning of the day we now call Easter. They had not come to see him alive, they had come to do the final, loving act of embalming him — last rites for the one they

had loved. There they go, the Passover is ended now —
going to the grave site — going to do what they can —
but it is too late for that ... He has already RISEN!

This act would never have been done for Christ if Mary
of Bethany had not done it earlier, aforetime — you could
almost say she actually embalmed him while he was still
alive!

May God grant us the same wisdom to work while we
have time and opportunity ... it will not always be ours.

DIVINE APPROBATION IS BEAUTIFUL

Mary's action did seem a bit illogical — and there were
"instant accusers." They called it a waste, they would
call it "religious fanaticism" today. But go ahead and
serve with devotion like hers and then listen carefully,
for you'll find the familiar voice speaking in your defense
as well: "Let her/him alone. That's beautiful!"
     And if he likes it ...
          that's plenty good enough for me!

The Little Miracle Before
The Big One

Scripture Reading: Luke 22:39-51

*And one of them struck the slave of the high priest
and cut off his right ear. But Jesus said, "No more of
this!" And he touched his ear and healed him.*
— *Luke 22:50-51*

If you were a Miracle-Worker, and you had one final
miracle to perform before dying, what would you choose
as a big, never-to-be-forgotten climax? Suppose you had
already done such things as calm a storm at sea, multiply
five loaves and two fishes into enough food to feed five
thousand people, walked on water, opened blind eyes,
caused the dumb to speak, the lame to walk, and the deaf
to hear, turned water into wine, and even raised the
dead — now you are about to do one more miracle before
you die — what would it be?

The last miracle Jesus performed before going to the
cross is pretty little in the light of all the spectacular
ones he has previously done. It happened something like
this: Jesus, and some of the disciples, are in the Garden
of Gethsemane, and the police have just arrived to arrest
him. Judas has pointed him out to the officers by plant-
ing a kiss of betrayal on his cheek. The enemies close in
to take him by force (as if they needed force when he is
"laying his life down of his own choosing") and Peter
jumps in (as usual), without thinking, starts swinging
with his sword, and lops off the ear of the slave of the
high priest. Peter was not trying to get at Malchus more
than any of the others, he is simply slashing, swinging,
stabbing in desperation — anything to protect Jesus. So
when the sword makes the critical contact with Malchus,

his right ear is severed from his head. Now Jesus has another job to do — he must correct the mistake made by one of his own men — for one of his enemies. This is the only biblical account that we have of a healing following an act of violence. The miracle involved here is not so much that Jesus could heal Malchus' ear — his ability is no longer in question — the real miracle is that he would do it! Jesus, on his way to the cross, takes time to stoop down and feel around in the dark — in the grass of the Garden of Gethsemane, retrieve the ear, and put it back on the head of its owner. A miracle-worker like that can be my Master any time!

There are some good lessons to be learned from the miracle before us.

THE MIRACLE OF MALCHUS SHOWS HOW TO TREAT YOUR ENEMIES

For about three and a half years, since the sermon on the Mount, Jesus has been preaching and teaching about how to treat your enemies. He said: "love your enemies," once he said: "if your enemy hunger, feed him." Another time he said "forgive your enemies," and again: "If your enemy smite you on one cheek; turn the other cheek." He taught no retaliation in anger, or hatred, or violence. Now, on the way to the cross. he is remembering what he taught, practicing what he preached!

Jesus seems to be the only one in the whole crowd who remembered how God expected him to act: The Jews were blind to God, Judas had abandoned God, the Disciples for the moment had forgotten God, but Jesus was the only one who remembered God.

The honest truth is that most of us, secretly, commend the action of Peter. We think it was a pretty good idea to start killing the enemy, if possible. After all, we think,

"Peter was only being loyal to Jesus, and besides Malchus deserved to get hurt for what he was doing."

Our well-intentioned, un-Christian actions are in direct disobedience to the Spirit that Jesus had and taught. He taught us to love the unloveable, to be compassionate to the ugly. It is a terrible indictment against us all for our failure to follow his teachings more closely, when it is said that the atheist, Madelyn Murray O'Hare, has said, "I never met a Christian who did not hate me."

The sad fact is that revenge is pretty attractive to most of us yet. A story is told of a small, timid man sitting in a local bar, minding his own business, when a big bully of a man walked over to him, chopped him across the neck, knocked him down and said, "That's Karate, I got it in Korea." The small fellow didn't say a word, just picked himself up and sat back down. Soon the big guy returned, came up to the little fellow, grabbed him up and out of his chair, threw him over his shoulder a couple of times, finally pinned him to the floor, looked the man in the face and said, "That's Judo, I got it in Japan." The little guy, this time, got up and left the bar — but returned in a little while. He walked up behind the big bully, cracked him with a terrible blow over the head, knocked him unconscious, and when he came to consciousness about a half hour later the little man was standing over him saying: "That's a crowbar, I got it at Sears!"

Contrast that way of dealing with your enemies with the true story of a sheepman in Indiana who was troubled by his neighbors' dogs who were killing his sheep. Sheepmen usually counter that problem with lawsuits, barbed wire fences, or even shotguns — but this man went to work on his neighbors with a better idea. To every neighbor's child he gave a couple of lambs as pets, and in due time, when all his neighbors had their own small flocks, they began to tie up their dogs, and that put an end to the problem.

Another thing to note about this incident: Do you recall that Peter, who used his sword to cut off Malchus' ear, was one of the sleeping disciples? A short while before Jesus had called them into the garden to watch and pray with him. They had not prayed, but fallen asleep instead. How do you suppose Peter would have acted in this situation if he had prayed? Prayer makes you feel a lot differently about your enemies — and greatly affects how you treat them.

THE MIRACLE OF MALCHUS SHOWS JESUS' INTEREST IN SMALL PROBLEMS / PEOPLE

Imagine how many things Jesus had on his mind now — just think of the pressure. He has gone through the agony of the bloody-sweat in Gethsemane, he's been betrayed by one of his own disciples, he's on his way to false arrest and a mock trial, finally to face death by crucifixion on a cross — pretty big problems he had, don't you think? How can he be bothered at a time like this with a slave that is an enemy that happens to get his ear in the way of Peter's sword? Weightier matters are on his mind. But he took time to perform a miracle of healing for an enemy — and on the way to his own death!

Have you ever noticed that the needs of others come to us also at odd and inconvenient times? We would really like to help, to show our concern, but those problems always come when we are "too busy," "too tired," "it's our day off," "we are on vacation," "we just got to bed," or "we don't feel very well ourselves today" — people's needs never match the convenient times in our lives. The wonder of this miracle is that Jesus, with so much at stake, takes time for a small matter for a man no one else considers important, and an enemy at that! But nothing was ever too big or too little for his attention. This little miracle teaches us how anxious he is to help us, anytime, any place, and in any situation.

He had time to heal the ear of Malchus,
    time to look at Peter with eyes of forgiveness,
    time to pardon a thief on the cross,
    time to pray for all of us when dying.

A recent cartoon showed a Loan Department Officer bidding farewell to a disappointed couple, whom he had just refused a loan. The caption under the picture read: "Sorry, but I hope you'll try us again sometime when you don't need it quite so badly."

    Jesus would never do that to anybody, because he cares.

God is so concerned about us that he even keeps count of the numbers of the hairs on our head. Someone recently estimated that blondes have approximately 145,000 hairs, brunettes have 120,000 hairs, and red-heads approximately 90,000 hairs. That's a lot of hairs to keep track of! The Jews used to be so impressed with the individual attention of God that they claimed each blade of grass had its own guardian angel. God really does care about us, we DO matter to him!

    Don't you see that a God who heals the ear of an enemy,
    who counts hairs,
    who watches for fallen sparrows,
    who puts clothes on lilies, and
    who lights the stars at night ...
        can be trusted to handle all of the
        large and small matters of your life?

THIS LITTLE MIRACLE LIVES ON

We never hear of Malchus again — Scripture is silent about the rest of his life — but, just turn it around —

suppose it had been you — wouldn't you have laid down your sword, changed loyalties, and followed Jesus for the rest of your life?

When our daughter was a little thing, about three or four years old, she'd occasionally fall or hurt herself some way. I'd fix it up the best I could, then take her on my lap, hold her close and say: "Jodi, if I could choose any little girl in all the world — any size, any color, anywhere, no matter how much I had to pay for her — do you know who I'd choose?" She'd always reply, though she knew the answer, "No, who?" And then I'd say, "I'd choose you, Jodi, I'd pick you!" Then she would be real quiet for a little bit and then look up at me with her nearly-black eyes just shining and say: "Tell me again, mamma, tell me again!"

Could it have been that way with Malchus? We can't say for sure, so just consider a "parable" of Malchus with me: Malchus is aglow with a new knowledge. He's a slave (and that's not new), but now for the first time in his life he is important to someone. Someone who looks for his ear in the grass in the darkness — no one has ever thought he even mattered before. All he's been good for is to wait on someone else, to carry out an order, to do a job — no one has ever cared how he felt, what he thinks, what his troubles are — and now this one, he hears them call his name — Jesus — he cares, he notices his need and stops to fix it for him!

Malchus stands afar off on Good Friday and can hardly stand it, for his new Friend of only a few hours is dying — and finally breathes his last breath. With sinking heart, Malchus thought it was all over — and went home with a feeling inside him like he'd swallowed a heavy rock. He does his work numbly, his hopes — so short lived — dashed to pieces on a rugged Cross-tree set in a rock on a hill, and life becomes a drag again, only now it is worse than ever, for he now has tasted hope for the first time in his life, only to have it snatched from him while the taste of it is fresh in his mouth.

Then Sunday morning dawns — just another day — until he hears the news — his Friend is alive and well! Resurrected! And he thought to himself, "I should have known he could do it, that he would do it! I should have realized God would not let him die — to live no more!" And maybe, our parable says, Malchus became, forever after, a true disciple and follower of Christ.

And maybe Malchus had a small son, a son who was his pride and joy, a small boy whom he'd often take on his knees and tell him: "Son, feel my ear — no, not that one, the one on the right side. Do you know that ear one night lay in the grass — in the grass over there in Gethsemane — and Jesus, our Lord, put it back? Son, he fixed it so well that even to this day I hear better from it than I do from the other ear." And Malchus continues: "Son, don't ever forget that Jesus cares for you, too. Remember, when you grow up to be a man, even if you are a slave, nothing, nothing can ever happen to you that will not matter to him . . ." — and don't you suppose the son of Malchus looked up into his father's face, and with his face alight with hope and expectancy said, "Tell me again, daddy, tell me again!"

So here is this last miracle of Jesus, the little one, probably the smallest of them all, set in contrast against the largest miracle of all time — the miracle of Redemption.

Such a little miracle: He can stop to fix the ear of a slave, on the one hand — on the other, such a wondrous miracle that it affords salvation for a whole world! Now don't you think that you and your problems can fit in-between these two miracles somewhere . . . and Christ will handle them, too?